I0502619

Financial Security
in
Ten Steps

*Diversify, Create Multiple Streams of Income
and Retire a Millionaire*

By

Tommy Keith
The Unconventional Strategist

Author of
Start Grow Sell

Copyright © 2016 by Tommy Keith

The Unconventional Strategist

All rights reserved. This book or any portion thereof may not be reproduced or used in any manner whatsoever without the express written permission of the publisher except for the use of brief quotations in a book review.

ISBN-13:
978-1536815764

ISBN-10:
1536815764

ACKNOWLEDGEMENTS

Thank you to my amazing wife, Becky, for always being there for me through these forty-plus years of marriage and for allowing me to just be myself. I am truly blessed to have you in my life!

To my son Ryan, who patiently read this section-by-section as I attempted to capture this in a format that might be useful to a broader audience than originally planned - thank you!

My Dad, Ellis, taught me how to work hard and he taught me to tackle the hard problems head on – thank you!

I would like give special thanks to my editor, Sally-Anne Cleveland. I love that I can just write and know that you will make me sound so much better – thank you!

DISCLAIMER

This book is based solely on my personal experiences. I am not providing legal, contractual, or financial advice; I am sharing the story of my personal business and investing approach.

This book includes information that was current at the time of writing. I have done my best to be accurate, but websites change constantly.

CONTENTS

PREFACE

The year 2015 was a flat year for the stock market, and 2016 started off as the worst year *ever* for stocks. As I write this, I see huge drops in the stock market day after day and I am getting calls and emails from family and friends asking what they should do—hold their stocks? Sell? Take some profits? Move to cash?

I am not a financial adviser, but I get these calls and emails because I have spent the last twenty-plus years focusing on learning about investing and diversifying my personal investments so that I am, it is hoped, protected in times like these.

To be sure, I lose money on occasion because I do invest, but I am able to sleep comfortably at night because I have put a lot of time and energy into learning about investing and taking responsibility for my own investment decisions— something I would not have been prepared to do twenty years ago.

When I got out of the Air Force over twenty years ago at the age of thirty-nine, I realized that almost one-half to one-third of my working life was over. I had almost no savings or investments of significance and I had no real *plan* to achieve financial security. I had spent my years trying to be the best husband, father, and Air Force Airman I could, and I never really learned anything about finances or investing during those years. I always assumed achieving financial security and my eventual retirement were just too far off in my future to worry about while I was still in my twenties and thirties.

Boy, was I wrong.

To be more specific, when I got out of the Air Force I was 39 years old, married with three children, and I realized:

- We had almost no savings.

- We had very limited emergency funds.

- We were almost living paycheck to paycheck.

- We were one big emergency away from possible bankruptcy.

- We had engaged a broker three years before and he had not done anything to help us increase our net worth or prepare for market swings. Instead, he just lined his pockets with the fees he charged us.

- We had three children approaching college age and we had no funds saved to help them pay for college.

- We did not really understand investing.

- We lived in one of the most expensive cities in the country.

I took stock of my financial situation and I did not like what I saw. I did not like what I had accomplished (or, more accurately, what I had *not* accomplished) financially in my first twenty-plus years of working.

I saw myself repeating family history. I was not saving or really doing anything to achieve financial security. It worried me that I would end up living off of social security with little-to-no savings, and I would never be able to do the things I wanted to do most, which is travel and explore new things while I was healthy enough to do so.

As I wrote this last point, *while I was healthy enough to do so,* I was thinking of my mom. Mom was diagnosed with Alzheimer's at the age of sixty-five. Mom never got to enjoy retirement. I remember her talking over the years about all the places she would love to visit when Dad retired. But those travel days never came for her and Dad, thanks to that devastating disease.

I wanted to enjoy life *as I lived my life*, not spend my working years planning for a fun-filled retirement that may never come. But most importantly — truly most importantly to me — was that I always wanted financial security for my wife and family, and I started to feel, at the age of thirty-nine, that I would never be able to achieve the kind of financial security I wanted. It was a bit depressing and a bit overwhelming to think about.

I didn't really know what *financial security* meant; it was simply a term indicating I could retire carefree and with plenty of money to do what I wanted to do whenever I wanted to do it. I had my work cut out for me, as I really did not know where to begin or how to get started toward financial security.

~~~~~~

To jump ahead in time, I did figure things out and I have achieved financial security for my family. That is what this book is all about and why I wanted to write it. At the age of sixty-one, I am able to retire any time I want and I feel good about our financial situation. (I am just not ready to retire yet because I still enjoy what I do.) For the last several years I have been living my life as I choose to live it, and I am not waiting for *retirement* to do the fun things I want to do.

While I am writing this book for anyone who can benefit, I am writing *primarily* to my three children because I want them to take ownership of their lives and their financial security too. I want them to start even earlier in life than I did, to prepare for their financial security. I don't want them to approach forty years old in the same financial position I was in at that age.

I hope they will learn from me, create their own financial roadmap, and create their own financial security like I did. I hope everyone who reads this will agree to take ownership of his or her own financial security as well.

This book is *not* a get-rich-quick story. The bookstores are full of get-rich-quick stories, but my story is about getting my act together and becoming educated and focused on achieving financial security; it's about taking advantage of my remaining working years *without* having to save so hard that we could not enjoy life along the way.

There are two main reasons I wrote this book:

> 1. I want my children to understand they too *can* create their own financial security and enjoy life *as they live it.* They are in their early thirties and it won't be long before they will be reaching the age of forty — where I was when I finally realized that, financially, I was nowhere near where I needed to be to achieve financial security. While they have more time to prepare for financial security than I found myself with, I wanted to write this book for them so they could start preparing today.

> 2. I want to use some of the profits from this book to donate to The Lamb Center (www.TheLambCenter.org) in their mission of serving the poor and homeless. Please read the chapter entitled "Give Back" for more on The Lamb Center. My mother used to always read a book's introduction and the first and last chapters to decide if she really wanted to read the entire book; make sure you read "Give Back" even if you don't read every other chapter. But I really hope you will read this book from cover to cover and benefit from my life lessons.

Thank you in advance for buying and reading this book!

I know it is a bit presumptuous to think I will sell enough copies of this book to make a dent in the cost of The Lamb Center's mission this year (which includes raising enough funds to pay for a new multimillion-dollar facility to be able to expand its support to the ever-growing needs of the poor and homeless), but if you know me, you know I always set hard-to-achieve goals.

If you enjoy this book, I hope you will buy copies for your children and anyone else who is convinced they will never be able to achieve financial security and on their own terms. Buy this book for yourself, your loved ones, and your friends! I will sell this book through Amazon so it will be easy to find.

GETTING STARTED

In thinking about my wife, Becky, and our children, I knew I did not want to ever be in a situation where Becky and I were financially dependent upon our children to take care of us. I also knew I did not want to be in a situation where I had to rely on the government to care for us. I especially did not want to live paycheck to paycheck, where all I had was social security to get us through our retirement years.

Becky and I don't need to buy a lot of *things* to make us happy. Too many people live their lives assuming money, status, and popularity are the most important things in life and they live their entire working lives trying to get more money, gain more status, and become more popular. They prioritize money, status, and popularity over relationships and their own health. When they get to be my age, they realize they have made the wrong things priorities in life and they find themselves less happy and usually less healthy in general.

But what I personally want is to *enjoy life* with Becky, and I want to spend time with my family, my grandchildren, and my friends. I want to travel. I want to learn new things. I love to learn; learning drives me.

I want to live life on my terms and not be constrained by limited finances. And I don't want to live a life where I have too many *things* that require my attention and limit my flexibility to come and go as I want to. I want the flexibility and freedom to be able to pack and hit the road anytime Becky says she wants to go visit the grandchildren (or when I want to travel somewhere new — one of my favorite things to do besides playing with the grandchildren).

~~~~~

I have also learned that life is too short to live in fear. I want to live the rest of my life to its fullest and never be held back by fear as I was for so many of my younger years. I spent a good part of my life afraid of doing the wrong things, afraid of disappointing my parents, and then afraid of disappointing my employer, afraid of disappointing my wife, afraid of disappointing my children … and the list goes on and on.

In a strange way, I was actually afraid of living up to my own potential (or afraid of *not* living up to my own potential). For many years I did not even recognize the value of *me*.

Read the following and ask yourself what these words mean to you.

> *Our deepest fear is not that we are inadequate,*
>
> *our deepest fear is that we are powerful beyond measure.*
>
> *It is our light, not our darkness that frightens us.*
>
> *We ask ourselves, who am I to be brilliant, gorgeous, talented, fabulous?*
>
> *Actually, who are we not to be?*
>
> *You are a child of God.*
>
> *Your playing small doesn't serve the world.*
>
> *There's nothing enlightened about shrinking so that other people won't feel insecure around you.*
>
> *We are born to make manifest the glory of God that is within us.*
>
> *It is not just in some of us; it is in everyone.*
>
> *And as we let our light shine, we unconsciously give other people permission to do the same.*

As we are liberated from our fears, our presence automatically liberates others.

What was best-selling author Marianne Williamson saying to you as you read this?

Read it again now. I mean *really* read it. What is she saying to you?

I think she is saying to not be afraid to *be you*.

> Don't be afraid *of* you.
>
> Do *set yourself apart*.
>
> Don't be afraid to have a big vision and don't be afraid to achieve your vision. Don't be afraid of working hard toward your own vision.
>
> Don't model your life after others or what others decide is important and try to force upon you.
>
> Don't be afraid to try new things and don't be afraid to fail.

So, set fear aside. Set yourself apart. Set your own future. I have read more than once that everything you want is on the other side of fear.

I have to ask you, when will *you* decide what is important and when will you move past your fear and *get started living to your potential*?

~~~~~~

So how did I achieve financial security (besides just setting aside fear, which I admit was a major part)? I achieved *Financial Security in Ten Steps*:

Step 1: I Took Ownership of My Finances

Step 2. I Changed the Way I Looked at Money

Step 3. I Recognized I Could Not Learn Everything

Step 4. I Made a Commitment to Never Stop Saving and Investing

Step 5: I Dealt with My Debt

Step 6: I Started an Emergency Fund

Step 7: I Started a Company - Then I Started Other Companies

Step 8: I Diversified My Investments

Step 9: I Protected My Assets

Step 10: I Use Every Legal Tax Advantage I Can to Keep My Money

While doing Steps 1-10: We Gave Back.

As I mentioned in the Preface, this is not a get-rich-quick story. I am not a financial advisor and I am not offering financial advice; instead, this is *my story about how we got our act together and grew our net worth and achieved financial security with a focused plan* that we have executed over these last several years.

I learned and took full advantage of the concepts of *compound interest, diversification,* and the *time value of money.* I'll cover these topics in detail later, but you can do a simple web search on "time value of money" to learn what this means. A good starting place is the explanation and examples given on the Investopedia website:

http://www.investopedia.com/terms/t/timevalueofmoney.asp

I also learned the value of owning my own business and learning enough about finances to take over and manage my own investments (with the input and advice of others).

A primary financial focus for me over these last 20 years has been creating multiple streams of income to achieve financial security and carry us through our retirement years. Slow and steady saving, investing, and creating streams of income — diversified streams of income that will continue to provide financial security for the rest of our lives.

Everyone who knows us knows we are fairly simple people — fairly frugal and also pretty generous. Giving back generously is part of who we are, and we want to always be in a financial position to be able to give to our favorite charities.

So this book is my story. This book is our (Becky's and my) story. It has been a life of learning, saving, learning some more, relearning, investing, succeeding, failing, restarting and persistence, failing again, and giving back all along the way. I have learned to push through the fear that gripped me and held me back for so many years in so many ways.

While I am writing this for my three children, my hope is that anyone can benefit from what I have to say here. You don't have to follow my steps exactly. But you do need to do what I did: take stock of where you are, decide where you want to be, and then *just get started*. Go about creating and executing a plan to get you where you want to be, financially and in life.

You don't want to be approaching your retirement years and have to rely on Uncle Sam to provide for your daily needs. I know too many people who live on meager social security checks and have never saved up enough money to be able to do all the things they talked about doing all of their working years. I know too many people like my Mom, who, because of Alzheimer's, never lived to see and enjoy her retirement years.

Action Steps For You

I hope you will read this book from cover to cover and then put your own plan together. You can follow my steps or create your own, but I encourage you, right now, to at least read the following list and commit to achieving your own *Financial Security in Ten Steps*:

Take ownership of your finances (Step 1)

Change the way you look at money (Step 2)

Recognize that you cannot learn everything (Step 3)

Make a commitment to never stop saving and investing (Step 4)

Deal with your debt (Step 5)

Start an emergency fund (Step 6)

Start a company. Then start other companies (Step 7)

Diversify your assets (Step 8)

Protect your assets (Step 9)

Use every legal tax advantage you can to keep your money (Step 10)

STEP 1: TAKE OWNERSHIP OF YOUR FINANCES

Taking ownership of my finances involved taking stock of my financial situation, deciding where I wanted to be financially, and then figuring out how I would get to my financial targets.

I took stock of my own financial situation by borrowing from a well-known and very simple three-step approach to tackling almost any problem:

> A. Where are you?

> B. Where do you want to be?

> C. How will you get there?

So, let's look at each of these in order.

A. Where Are You?

My story begins when I got out of the Air Force at the age of thirty-nine and I realized that one-half to one-third of my working life was over and I had no real plan to achieve financial security

I realized:

- We had almost no savings

- We had very limited emergency funds.

- We were almost living paycheck to paycheck.

- We were one big emergency away from potential bankruptcy.

- We had engaged a broker three years before and he had done us no favors.

- We had three children approaching college age and we had no funds saved to help them pay for college.

- We did not really understand investing.

- We lived in one of the most expensive cities in the country.

I knew I wanted to do better financially. I knew I wanted to be financially independent when I retired, but I had no clue where to begin. So I did what I always do in situations like this: I decided to tackle my problem by breaking my problem into easy, manageable chunks. I like to follow the *KISS* (Keep It Simple, Stupid) principle, so I decided to proceed with this basic three-step approach:

A. Where are you?

B. Where do you want to be?

C. How will you get there?

Business and financial planners alike often use this three-step approach.

Up to this point I have addressed my own personal *A. Where are you?* In the next section, I will address my own personal *B. Where do you want to be?*

B. Where Do You Want To Be?

I had to think long and hard about where I wanted to be financially. In the most simple terms, I knew I wanted to retire carefree and with plenty of money so my family was well taken care of and so we could do whatever we wanted to do whenever we wanted to do it. We did not have to be *filthy rich*, but financially secure.

In the last section, I talked about where I was. As I took stock of my situation, I realized I not only did not like my financial situation, but I had no plan to get any closer to where I wanted to be — let alone where I needed to be.

I needed to focus my energy on B: *Where do you want to be?*

Over the years I have read (and I have found it to be true) that it helps if you can start with the end in mind so you know what you are working toward. I needed to put some thought into where I wanted to be in the future (B) and come up with something of substance that I could define and work toward. I knew I would have to worry about *how I would get there* (C) later.

I started addressing where I wanted to be in the future (B) by setting some high-level *goals*.

I knew I wanted:

- Financial security for my family. (I basically guessed we would need at least a few million dollars so we would be truly self-sufficient.)

- To be able to help my children get a college education if they chose to go to college.

- To travel.

- To own a home Becky really loved.

- To be able to retire on my timeline *while I was healthy enough to enjoy retirement.*

- To be able to give generously of our time and money.

I also knew I did *not* want:

- To retire with limited-to-no savings.

- To have to survive and depend on social security or the government for my daily needs.

- My wife to have to live on social security or rely on the government to carry her through retirement should something happen to me.

I know this does not seem like a lot in terms of B. *Where do you want to be?* At least it was a *start* at defining where I wanted to be even if only at the broadest level. I knew I could add more substance to my B goals as I continued to work on my plan of attack. To be honest, some would argue that those bullet points don't even meet the criteria of the definition of *goals*, but for me and for the purpose of just getting started, this was good enough.

C. How Will You Get There?

Deciding what I wanted — just writing it out — only scared me even more, and once again I started thinking I did not even know where to begin. I thought I was too far along at the age of thirty-nine to be able to catch up, let alone meet or exceed my goals.

So like most people who are confronted with something that seems beyond their reach, my first step was to do nothing. My list of bullet points — my *goals* — seemed impossible to reach given that I'd spent twenty years working in the Air Force and I had accomplished almost nothing financially. I just did not see how I could accumulate enough money in the working years I had left to achieve true financial and financial security (especially given that we had saved so little the first twenty years of our working lives).

~~~~~~

At work I have always been a big-picture person, and thinking that way had always worked well for me. Yet *this* big picture (my goals, especially the idea of saving a few million dollars) seemed impossible to achieve.

But being the big-picture person I am, I sat down and wrote this simple personal *model*.

Make Money:

- Pay God

- Pay Taxes but Minimize Taxes

- Pay Ourselves – Save Some - Invest Some

- Pay the Bills

- Live on the Rest

- Give Back

As we *Pay Ourselves* (above), save until we can create a **second** stream of income, and from that:

- Pay God

- Pay Taxes but Minimize Taxes

- Pay Ourselves – Save Some - Invest Some

- Pay the Bills

- Live on the Rest

- Give Back

As we *Pay Ourselves* (above), save until we can create a **third** stream of income, and from that:

- Pay God

- Pay Taxes but Minimize Taxes

- Pay Ourselves – Save Some - Invest Some

- Pay the Bills

- Live on the Rest

- Give Back

Continue the above process and continue to create multiple streams of income for the rest of my life.

I did not know it at the time, but this simple model was to become the basis for my savings and investing and business model that we have lived and operated under ever since.

~~~~~~

But even more importantly, my model, my overarching approach, was to *focus my energy into diversified investments* that would hopefully, collectively, make money for me all day, every day, while protecting us from any one-investment failure.

I wanted to concentrate my energy on things that would hopefully always have the potential of providing an ongoing stream of revenue so that I could essentially make money while I slept.

Becky and I have never focused on accumulating *things* just to have things. Instead, we try to focus on things that will, in the end, grow in value and allow us to create from that even more value (more investment streams).

Said in its most simple terms, I became determined to become the best provider I could for my wife and family. It has never been about becoming rich for the sake of being able to say we are rich. What has driven me (us) has been the desire to live life on our own terms and not be dependent upon our kids or the government to take care of us. That will always drive us.

~~~~~~

It was this simple model that I have stuck with over the last several years to create my multiple streams of income and achieve our financial security. At the highest level (big picture), my plan was simply to create multiple streams of income that would provide financial security for us for life.

This plan as you have read it described here is so simple it is almost embarrassing. But as a big-picture guy, I always try to simplify things to their most basic level and then I drill down from there and create action steps. So I needed to put this simple model into action for the long term for it to be effective.

I have become a big believer in *reducing financial risk by diversifying* my streams of income, and I'll discuss this point throughout this book.

So, I Had a Plan...Sort of

Stepping back a bit to my *plan*, having a *plan* is always a great place to start, but then I was faced with how to turn my *simple plan* into *real* financial security for my family.

Or, said differently, how would I *really* go from where I was (A) to where I wanted to be (B) — and what actionable steps would I need to take (C)?

Step A was *defined*. Step B was *sort of defined*. Step C was the toughest part for me.

In reality, my model probably will never have an ending since I may never really retire ... or at least, retire the way most people think of retiring. Right now I can't imagine stopping my work, because I love what I do. Sure, I have my good days and I have some days where I just want to be a grandpa and not do anything work-related. But I always get pulled back to my work because it is a work environment that I created and I want to stay involved in. I created my own business model and I still have ownership in my companies, and, to be honest, I just like what I do. It is not really work. It is not a normal 8-5 job. Today's working environment does not have to be like the old days I grew up in where you join a company and you stay loyal to that company for 40 years and then you retire with a pension. More and more people are changing jobs, changing companies, and starting their own companies today than ever before. That is the path I chose.

~~~~~

The good news is, because of the choices Becky and I have jointly made over the years, retirement is finally our choice.

I do not have to work if I don't want to. Becky does not have to work if she does not want to. Some day I may decide that I'm done with work and just want to travel and play with my grandchildren. That will by my choice. That's where you want to be too. That's the financial security you want to have.

I will always be trying to find new ways to create new streams of income; it seems to be in my blood, and so it would really be a major change for me to not be doing what I currently love to do.

Your challenge is to create and use your own model or use my basic model and create multiple streams of income so you too can stop working on your own timeline with financial security for your family.

You will see over and over in this book that I'm a strong believer in diversifying. That is because I've seen too many times over the years where people were overly dependent on one retirement stream of income, only to be let down as their retirement stream lost income potential or went away completely. You've heard it said many times that you should not put all of your eggs in one basket. When it comes to your financial security, the same principle applies. Never put all of your retirement income into one basket that could go away for reasons out of your control. I'll discuss this more in upcoming chapters.

~~~~~~

Back to my simple model, it really is as simple as A-B-C. But one of the points I will drive home over and over again is that the earlier you get started, the better for you! As a review,

> **Step A: Where are you?** At the age of thirty-nine, I was not even close to financial security.

> **Step B: Where do you want to be?** I wanted financial security, but I needed to better define what financial security would look like for us.

> **Step C: How will you get there?** I needed to create actionable steps to get me to financial security.

I knew Step A fairly well and I only knew at a basic level what Step B meant or would look like. It was easy to seek financial security, but what did financial *security* really mean? I could easily say in one sentence that I wanted financial security, but I could not quantify what financial security meant. Since I had no idea of what Step C would involve, I decided to tackle this one step at a time.

I also realized that I would not — could not — come up with a *fixed plan*. I would need to have a plan that would evolve over time. That is one lesson I learned from my years in the Air Force where I heard the expression (over and over again), "Flexibility is the key to airpower." That applies in financial planning as well. You need to have a plan, but you need to recognize that the world is ever changing and you need to be flexible too.

~~~~~

Starting with the end (my Step B) in mind, I added these assumptions:

- I assumed that *if* social security still existed when I retired, social security would only be icing on the cake for us. In other words I could not and would not count on social security as a major component of my financial security. I just do not trust the government to manage social security and keep it fundamentally sound.

- I would have a net worth in the millions of dollars.

- Our house would be paid off and the maintenance taken care of by someone else.

- I would have multiple streams of income to replace my pre-retirement take-home pay.

Next, the hard part, I knew I had to put *more shape* to Step C. I knew I had to take personal ownership of this problem and the action plan because no one else could do this for me. I knew I would need to involve Becky every step of the way or to the extent she was interested. Becky tends to be risk-averse and has always adopted the attitude of "I'll trust you with our finances, just keep me in the loop and informed." I am the risk taker, so Becky and I balance each other pretty well.

~~~~~~

To begin with (and remember, this was over twenty years ago), I decided that at a minimum, my portfolio would include a mix of:

- Retirement accounts

- Investments outside of retirement accounts

- Real estate ownership

This diversification (especially *investments outside of our retirement accounts*) was important for several reasons. We wanted a fallback plan in case one element faltered. Many people have worked their entire lives and have never really saved because they are counting on social security and their pension to carry them through retirement.

Now, with fewer and fewer companies offering pensions, people have to come up with their own financial security portfolio like I did. I believe each person should create his own financial security portfolio. Each portfolio should include a diversified set of investments that provides multiple streams of income. You and your spouse should work together to create a balanced and diversified set of investments together that works for both of you.

I use more than one retirement account as part of my portfolio. But I worry that not enough people are saving enough in their retirement accounts to really carry them through retirement. I worry that even my own children are not already focused on their financial security, because like me at their age, they are focused on life and work and family — not their future.

On the other hand, I worry that some people are putting too much money into their retirement accounts and not keeping enough accessible cash on hand when they want to buy a house or get themselves through an emergency period.

You don't want to put so much into your retirement accounts that you don't have the cash on hand when you need it and the last thing you want to do is to have to borrow from your retirement accounts every time you need cash. You will pay hefty fees when you borrow from your retirement accounts.

So, balance is key! Find a way to, over the long term, fund your retirement accounts while building cash and a diversified portfolio outside of your retirement accounts.

I Realized I Could Figure Things Out

Somewhere along the way, I realized I *did know enough* to figure things out. I *did know enough* to put together an executable financial security plan of my own.

Sometimes *just getting started* helps and makes you realize that you *do know enough* after all to at least put a plan in place that you can start acting against. I started feeling a little better, but I knew I had a long way to go. Thank goodness I had more than twenty years to get to my desired Step B and financial security.

~~~~~

I had a college degree. In fact, I had received a Bachelor of Science degree in Electrical Engineering, and I later received a Master of Science degree in Electrical Engineering with a specialty in radar and digital systems design. So I knew I wasn't stupid, and I knew I could figure out a solution to my financial problem if I would just put my mind to it; I just had not put my mind to it. I realized that if I could complete my electrical engineering degrees, then I *should* be able to figure out a solution to my quest for financial security.

This was *step one* once I had admitted I had never really taken *ownership* of my financial security. It was time to do just that though. No one else would — no one else could. I had to do this for me. I had to do this for us. *I had to learn about investing.* Given that I had no education in finances or investing, that made me a bit nervous.

I had to create an action plan, and as I said before, I knew it would be an ever-evolving action plan.

> *The way to get started is to quit talking and begin doing.* — Walt Disney

So I wrote down these specific steps I had to begin working on immediately ... and possibly repeat for the rest of my life:

- Learn about money and investing.

- Learn about real estate.

- Live below our means.

- Put my raises in the bank.

- Reduce debt.

- Build and keep an emergency fund.

- Learn from others.

- Read everything I could to learn my options to achieve financial security.

I also realized I needed to address my *self-talk* regarding our finances. I told myself:

- I was smart enough to learn *what I needed to know.*

- I could not learn it all, but *I could learn enough.*

- I could never give up.

- I had to constantly remind myself I did have enough time left in my working years, even though it seemed impossible at the time.

So I read everything I could read in my spare time and we kept pressing on and we kept saving every year while we learned more and more about investing.

Don't Be Afraid to Have a Big Vision for Your Own Financial Security Plan

When my children were growing up they were always saying, *I want* this, or, *I want* that. They thought the world existed to satisfy their every need.

If they don't remember, I certainly do, and I promise they were constantly saying, *I want …!*

They didn't think twice about asking for it, demanding it, or just taking it, because they were just like every other child: they wanted it and that was good enough for them.

For the purposes of this book and your financial visioning:

Don't be afraid to let that little child in you come out. Let that little child *take over* and help you create your financial vision. Think big! Create a vision so large that it seems out of reach.

> *If your vision doesn't scare you, then both your vision and your God are too small.* — Brother Andrew

I believe if you set a modest vision, you will most likely not achieve all that you have the *potential to achieve.* The same for your savings and financial security planning: if you set a modest plan, then you will probably achieve a modest result, but you will most likely not achieve all that you could have achieved if you had set your vision higher!

> *The greater danger for most of us lies not in setting our aim too high and falling short; but in setting our aim low, and achieving our mark.* — Michelangelo

In fact, having a vision larger than what you can currently deliver on will actually, in the long run, be the best way to ensure that you meet your goal. A *larger vision will stretch you* and it will challenge you.

There are a lot of websites and books you can read and learn you how to create your own vision, but I decided to do what a child would do and just come up with a long list of *I want* statements as the *start of my vision.* So, at the age of thirty-nine, I found a quiet corner where I would not be interrupted and I just wrote everything that came to my mind — unfiltered. I wrote simple statements that collectively became the basis of the vision I would work toward. That vision had many parts and there were things that at the time would seem almost impossible to achieve. These are some of the *vision (I want) statements* I wrote down early in my planning stages:

- I will never work *for* anyone *ever* again.

- I will truly *become my own boss.*

- I will create financial security for my family.

- I will be able retire when I want to retire.

- I will create multiple streams of income that will sustain my family.

- I will become a multimillionaire.

- I will have a diverse set of investments that protect my family from worst-case scenarios.

- I will enjoy life and travel when I want to and not wait until I am too old or physically unable to travel.

- I will give back not only my money, but from my various resources and God-given talents.

- I will get in shape and stay physically fit.

Since vision statements evolve and grow, it wasn't long before I added things like:

- I will own my own company.

- I will own more than one company.

- I will own real estate … not just my home.

Did you notice that I said *I will* in each case?

I had to decide what **I** wanted my future to look like and I knew that **I** had to take ownership of my vision and **I** had to be the one to make sure **I** achieved my vision. No one else would! No one else could!

YOU will need to decide what you want **YOUR** future to look like. **YOU** will need to take ownership of **YOUR OWN** vision. **YOU** have to be the one to make sure **YOU** achieve **YOUR** vision.

Action Steps for You

1. Why don't you stop reading right now and remember what it was like to be a child, and write your own *I want* statements?

Don't be afraid to be bold and creative, and don't worry about what anyone might think about your *I want* statements. Shut down all of those crazy voices in your head that tell you *You can't* or *You shouldn't* or any other voices that limit your child-like *I want* brainstorming.

My vision statements (my *I want* statements) have changed somewhat over the years, and yours will most likely change too, so don't let yourself or the world *filter* your huge vision statements (your *I want* statements).

Some people will write one very complete vision statement that they hope to achieve, and that is okay; I just wanted to write down multiple statements that captured the various aspects of my thinking.

It is up to you how you go about writing your vision for your financial future; the key thing is that YOU write your own vision statement or statements.

If you didn't stop and write your own thoughts down when I mentioned it a few paragraphs back, please do it now. Stop and just be like the child you used to be and write something down now. It does not have to be perfect; the point is to write whatever comes to mind. Do it now! Even if you have to do this over a few days, take the time to do this critical step.

Why did I repeat this? Because most people will read books like this and, in the end, that's all they will do. They won't act on what they read or they think they will come back and compete the steps at a later date. The truth is, most do not *ever* come back and act on what they read.

That is one way you can be different from the majority of the readers. You can choose to **act** and not just read.

Financially responsible and successful people don't achieve their vision and build their wealth by accident and they don't build it overnight. You need to think big and have some serious willpower to reach that big vision. You have to be able to keep your eye on the prize of financial security; often that means you must be willing to sacrifice your present *wants* for the sake of your future.

The more I read and the more I strategized and planned, the more I started to change the way I looked at money.

2. Now, reread this A-B-C list and *think* about the answer to each question (even if only at the highest level at first):

>   A. Where are you today?

>   B. Where do you want to be?

>   C. How will you get there?

3. Next, read each question again, but this time *write down* whatever comes to mind as you answer each question.

For now, just get something down on paper or in your computer and then review it every day for a few days and edit your answers until they take shape. Keep your updated answers close by as you read this book and update your answers as ideas come to you. There is nothing wrong with refining your answers over time.

As part of your answers, write your own *I will* statements. Write down as many *I will* statements as you need to, and add to your list as they come to you. I promise that once you start this practice, you will continue to think of new *I will* statements and you will be refining your list over time.

Draft your own vision of where you want to be financially (and a general timeline for your vision).

It's as simple as **A-B-C!**

STEP 2: CHANGE THE WAY YOU LOOK AT MONEY

I used to be afraid of money and investing. I did not really understand money or investing and I avoided trying to figure it out because I always believed if I ever saved enough money I could just hire someone to manage it for me. This was a mistake, as I'll explain throughout this chapter and this book.

Up until I was thirty-nine years old, I really had no financial investing training and I never read business or investing books.

I think a lot of people are a lot like I was: they have no formal training in finances or in investing and they get so wrapped up in the day-to-day aspects of just living their lives that they never take the time to learn about money or investing. We are all taught to just do a great job at work and if you are fortunate enough to save up some money then you can just hire someone else to be your financial advisor.

I have since become an avid reader about investing and business and it was really through my personal reading that I started to change the way I looked at money and investing — and I began to have less fear of money and investing.

I hope you will be different too and I hope you will read and learn about money and investing. I hope you will apply what you learn in this book and then *take ownership of your own money and financial decisions*.

Most people just end up relying on financial advisors (or friends) to guide and advise them on their finances and investing options — and quite often they rely on *financial experts* to make decisions *for* them.

That was how I did things until a little over twenty years ago. Yes, I still rely on advisors and yes I still have so much to learn, but I make the decisions now in concert with my wife after considering the advice of others. I admit, Becky still relies on me quite a bit to understand the finances, but I encourage her to be aware and be a part of all aspects of our finances.

I find it odd that understanding money and understanding investing is so critical to everyone's long-term well-being and their financial security, and yet most people do not even take the time to learn the basics.

Money and investing can be intimidating, so often, people like me (for the first thirty-nine years of my life) don't even try to learn the basics. I decided I wanted to be different, so I started reading all kinds of self-help and investing books trying to glean even a few golden nuggets that I could apply to my life and my own finances and better prepare for financial security.

But the more I read the more I struggled with knowing what *specifically to do*. So many of the books I read were great self-help books that talked *in general* about get-rich concepts, but never really helped me to understand *specifically what I could and should do* in any priority order.

Some books, though, were very helpful in *changing the way I looked at money*. I could never list every investing, business, or self-help book I've read, but I do want to share a few book titles that did help change and shape my way of thinking about money and investing. You will not find these books on today's top-ten list since they have all been out in print for several years. You can probably find many in your local library. As you read the books, just do what I did and focus on pulling key points that might apply to your situation.

I've always read each book with the goal of trying to pull one or more golden nuggets that I could apply to my situation. The reality is, a lot of 200-page books could be summarized in twenty or fewer useful pages, so you should learn to read with the intent of finding the golden nuggets that will work for you, and then apply those to your own situation. (It's not enough to just read and learn — you *have* to apply those lessons to your situation.) I realize the authors make their living selling books and want to appeal to as broad an audience as possible, so a lot of what they talk about in their books may never apply in my specific situation; the key for me was to pull out those lessons from each book that would work for me, and you should do the same.

One of the best (what I would call self-help) books I have ever read is *The Power of Focus* by Jack Canfield, Mark Victor Hansen, and Les Hewitt.

After reading it cover to cover the first time, I made it a point to reread this book every year for several years (I still skim through parts of it every year) because it has been so instrumental in helping me get to where I am — which is *a lot more focused in life*. This book is an easy read, but it is up to you to act on what you read in the book.

Am I the wealthiest individual in the world? No, I'm far from the richest in terms of dollars, but I have achieved some financial success and I live the balanced life that I chose. I live and work on my schedule (with Becky's input, of course). Long ago I gave up living my life by other people's rules and I gave up working to make others rich. I now work for us to make our lives better. The even better news is, I can retire anytime I want to … it is **my** choice.

The cover of *The Power of Focus* says, "What the World's Greatest Achievers Know About THE SECRET to Financial Freedom & Success."

The authors define their purpose in writing the book by borrowing a quotation from J. Paul Getty: "The individual who wants to reach the top in business must appreciate the might of the force of habit—and must understand that practices are what create habits. He must be quick to break those habits that can break him—and hasten to adopt those practices that will become the habits that help him achieve the success he desires."

Read that last paragraph again.

The authors went on to *guarantee* that if you study and gradually implement the strategies they share in the book, then you will not only hit your business, personal, and financial targets consistently—you'll far exceed the results you are now achieving.

Wow! That is quite a promise, but when I read the book the first time I breezed through it as if it were the usual bunch of fluff you read in every self-help book. Little did I know the impact this simple-to-read (and reread) book would have on my life.

Let me give you an overview of the book; then, go buy it and read it yourself and you will understand why I listed this book first. In a nutshell, the authors give you **Ten Focusing Strategies** to consider and outline *action steps* to implement these strategies into your daily life.

Focusing Strategy #1: Your Habits Will Determine Your Future. The authors talk about how habits work, how to identify bad habits, how to change bad habits, and how to create your own successful habits formula. This is one of the most important chapters in the book and it is worth reading and rereading.

Focusing Strategy #2: It's Not Hocus-Pocus, It's All About Focus. This chapter is all about learning to focus and keeping your focus. This chapter has helped me tremendously.

Focusing Strategy #3: Do You See the Big Picture. This chapter is all about learning to see and focus on the big picture. Most people spend their lives in the weeds or on lower-level details. You need to set your own path by creating — and writing down — your own vision of what the future will look like for you and then setting goals to work toward to make your vision a reality.

Focusing Strategy #4: Creating Optimum Balance. This chapter is about creating the optimum balance for you. Balance involves many things, including: creating a blueprint for your future, taking the right action, learning, exercising, relaxing, and allowing yourself enough think time.

Focusing Strategy #5: Building Excellent Relationships. This chapter is all about building the right relationships, learning to say *no* to the toxic people in your life, and finding great mentors.

Focusing Strategy #6: The Confidence Factor. To build your confidence, it helps to eliminate fear and worry, resolve unfinished business, forgive and forget, and create a winning attitude.

Focusing Strategy #7: Ask for What You Want. A lot of what you want you may never get simply because you never asked for it. So learn to ask for what you want.

Focusing Strategy #8: Consistent Persistence. Success is right around the corner when you learn about the benefits of consistency and actually are consistent in executing your vision. How many times have you just given up in the past? To get what you want you need to learn consistent persistence.

Focusing Strategy #9: Taking Decisive Action. Learn about active decision-making and become a problem solver.

Focusing Strategy #10: Living on Purpose. In this chapter, you wrap up all that you have learned in the book and learn to make your life simple again, to live on purpose, and to succeed.

I love that every chapter has **action steps** for you to work on. This is not a read-it-and-set-it-aside book. It is, in many ways, a workbook to help you achieve your vision.

The final section of the book says, "It's Your Life ... Accept the Challenge!"

This is my challenge to you: go buy and read *The Power of Focus* from cover to cover. Be sure to complete the action steps at the end of the chapters and then read the book again every year or so. Accept the authors' challenge and take action and *live on purpose.*

This book has changed the way I look at money. It was instrumental in helping me get past my fear of money and investing and actually start to create *action steps* I needed to get me focused and get my finances on track.

A question you have to ask yourself is, *What will you focus your energy on from now on?* Another question is, *When will you get started?*

~~~~~~

Years ago I read *Multiple Streams of Income: How to Generate A Lifetime of Unlimited Wealth* by Robert Allen.

While this 300+ page book is older, it still has a lot of useful information, some of which I have used. It also has some sections that I will never be able to use in my personal situation. This book covers many topics and is meant to be tailored to your own specific situation.

——

So what was important for me was to understand the *concepts* enough to be able to pull together and apply those that could work for me.

The introduction to the book drew me in right away when it outlined what I could learn from the book:

- A simple system for controlling your finances.

- How to invest your surplus funds without losing sleep at night.

- How to create multiple streams of lifetime income.

- How to oversee your growing financial empire in as little as ten minutes a day.

- How to leave a financially secure future to your family and loved ones.

While I knew this book could not possibly be the one-stop answer shop for everything I needed to know, it did answer a lot of my questions and it *got me started* in much more detail on my quest to *diversify* and *create multiple streams of lifetime income*. This book changed the way I looked at money.

The book challenges you, the reader, to add at least one new stream of income to your life each year, and it spends a lot of time helping you understand ways to do just that. I did not follow each step in the book, but I caught on to the idea of creating new streams of income and I have been creating diverse streams of income ever since.

You probably noticed the logo on title page of my books, the logo of the seedlings. This Robert Allen book reminds you that each dollar bill is a money seed. The question only becomes, how will you spend or invest your seeds. If you are like most people, you will overspend and over-leverage; I hope you will be different — invest, plant seeds, diversify.

Einstein said it best: "The most powerful invention of man is compound interest." If you just divert a few of your ill-spent dollars and funnel them into some well-timed investments, you can achieve financial success. — Robert Allen

This book emphasizes some of the most basic concepts that I have tried to follow and which I want to pass on to my own children: "Live on less than you earn. Invest the surplus. Avoid Debt." I would add to that point, "and *give back* all along the way."

I'll just share a few more points from the book and then I hope you will find time to read it—yes, it is an older book and some of it is outdated, but the key concepts will always be current and relevant.

Robert Allen talks a lot about seven essential *money skills* that you should think about:

- Value it.

- Control it.

- Save it.

- Invest it.

- Make it.

- Shield it.

- Share it.

He emphasizes these four points of wisdom that I agree with:

- The necessity for work: When you earn it, you value it.

- The importance of charity: Give away the first 10 percent.

- The need for saving: Give yourself the next 10 percent.

- The power of accountability: Account for every penny.

I hope I have piqued your interest. Robert Allen has several other books that are also worth reading; just search his name on Amazon and you can skim through the many books and workbooks he has authored. Robert Allen also wrote *Creating Wealth* and *The One Minute Millionaire*; both are good reads.

One thing I like about Robert Allen's book is that it is not a get-rich-quick scheme. It is just a book about watching how you spend every dollar, investing, monitoring, diversifying through multiple steams of income, and securing your financial future *while protecting all of your assets.*

~~~~~~

I mentioned before that I read books with the idea of learning one or more golden nuggets that will help me to grow. At first, I completely avoided books with titles like the following:

The Millionaire Maker: Act, Think, and Make Money the Way the Wealthy Do by Loral Langemeier.

But avoiding books based on title was wrong, because I found I could almost always find lessons to apply to our personal situation. I think I used to feel guilty about wanting to read these books because it almost seemed greedy to me to want to become a millionaire. I was not brought up to think like that and it just seemed wrong. But over time I changed my mindset to quit thinking about becoming a millionaire and instead started thinking more about achieving financial security for my family.

Langemeier helped to change the way I looked at money. I finally decided I would not be intimidated by money or millionaires and I would not feel guilty about trying to become a millionaire. I followed her advice to learn to *think like a millionaire and refine my own action plan to help me get on my path to my own financial security.*

I have to admit, I, like many of you reading this book, used to hear in church that money was the root of all evil. I can't tell you how many times I heard that growing up. But for years, I listened to those pastors talk about how money was evil, but I never noticed that the Bible (King James Version) says:

> *For the love of money is the root of all evil: which while some coveted after, they have erred from their faith, and pierced themselves through with many sorrows. — 1 Timothy 6:10*

It is the *love of money* that is the problem.

For me, it was never about the love of money; it was about achieving financial security. Langemeirer helped me to understand that there are certain characteristics and practices belonging to a lot of millionaires that can be understood and modeled and applied in your own life. If you want to achieve financial security, then model the behavior of those who have achieved financial security.

So for me, I had already accepted that I *could* learn to make a lot of money, and making a lot of money was not a problem if I did not fall into the *love of money* trap and err from my faith.

Langemeirer takes you the next step and teaches you about the cycle of money and an approach to map your way to millions. Langemeirer teaches you about sequencing and doing the right thing in the right order when it comes to investing. She teaches you about how to use your assets to create income and how to use entities to get your own house in order and grow even more rich through the use of entities that you can set up (as I have done several times now).

I won't go into more detail here; instead, search for her name on Amazon and buy the book yourself or go to your library and find the book and read it. Remember — and this is very important—don't get hung up on the numbers she uses in her examples. Focus on learning the *concepts* she is trying to teach you and then apply those concepts to your own life (like I have done).

~~~~~~

I also thoroughly enjoyed many of the books by Thomas Stanley because they too helped me to think differently about money. I *can* be a millionaire and *keep my faith* and I can use my resources to do good things. It helps to understand how others made their money and what set them apart. Some of Thomas Stanley's books include:

The Millionaire Mind

The Millionaire Next Door: The Surprising Secrets of America's Wealthy

Stop Acting Rich … and Start Living Like a Real Millionaire

You've heard the expression, "Don't reinvent the wheel!" The reason you want to read each of these books and so many other books like them is so you can learn how other people made their money and learn how they protected their money.

That is why I believe you too should read a diverse set of books and always be reading and learning from successful people. If you want financial security, then why reinvent the wheel? Learn from others who have done it before. Read! Read a lot of books!

~~~~~~

I have probably read every book Jim Cramer has written because he, more than any other author, has helped change the way I look at money.

For example, I have read:

Confessions of a Street Addict

Real Money: Sane Investing in an Insane World

Get Rich Carefully

Stay Mad for Life

Getting Back to Even

Cramer made me realize and accept that *I have to take ownership of my investments and my finances.* I cannot rely on anyone else to do my homework and to make the hard decisions. Well, I could rely on others, but I choose not to. I did not like the results when I did rely on others to make my financial decisions.

There are so many things I have learned from reading Cramer's books that I could never list everything here, so let me highlight just some of his key teachings.

Cramer says you need to take an active hand in setting yourself up for your retirement; you have to get involved with your money. Cramer says that even if you are only 20 years old, you should still start preparing for your eventual retirement now. He said you can put your money into a tax-deferred vehicle like a 401(k) or individual retirement account, and both are good options, but they are just a start. You also need to diversify and focus on other investments too, not just your 401(k) or other retirement account. Often 401(k)'s are limited in what you can invest in and make diversifying harder for some.

A key point Cramer was making here is that you need to have a balanced and diversified approach to retirement planning. Some people don't prepare at all for retirement and never save or invest. Others go the opposite extreme and put *everything* they can into retirement accounts and then when they need cash for everyday living expenses or emergencies they don't have cash they need, so they borrow and they pay interest — and they repeat this cycle all their lives. You need to find a happy middle ground where you save and invest and grow your available cash reserves (and emergency funds) to carry you through life.

Cramer also helped me to understand that when it comes to investing, it can be a mistake to be *too cautious*. Some books recommend that retirement money should be handled with low risk. But people often lose out by investing in the lower risk stocks or stock funds and never see the returns they could otherwise get with stocks or stock funds that carry more risk. This is especially true if you have many years until your retirement. You can afford to take more risks if you are younger because you have time on your hands to make up for potential losses. Often the reward for taking risks is far more profitable than being conservative and low risk. I do understand, though, that the closer you are to retirement, the more cautious you need to be with your assets and your investing.

Cramer says over and over again in his books and on his television show that you should *not* keep too much of your money in the company that employs you. More specifically, Cramer recommends that you never put more than a fifth of your retirement money into the stock of the company that employs you. You *must diversify* your portfolio and you should also never put too much money in just a few particular stocks. Imagine if you lost all of your retirement money because you over-invested in your company stock and the company went under for some reason. Think Enron! What a disaster for so many people when that company went under.

Many people currently take advantage of their 401(k) by having automatic monthly equal deductions from their paycheck. This way they don't have to think about it, and the money passively (hopefully) piles up. I used to do this myself.

Cramer is not a fan of this idea because the market is not the same every month. He argues, why invest the same amount of money every month, if there will be times when the market is better or worse? Now that I've learned enough about investing and how the market works, I do not use the automatic deduction approach. But I do understand why most people follow this approach. It is easy to do and they are at least putting something away each month. But when you are investing for retirement, when you have a really long time horizon, stock market pullbacks are opportunities to "Buy! Buy! Buy!" as Cramer says. Investing the same amount each month in your retirement account whether the market if going up or down just does not make sense to me (now). When there is a large percentage decline in the stock market, Cramer says you should take advantage and invest more.

He also recommends first investing in one or more low-cost S&P 500 index funds or an actively managed fund that operates like an index fund. Investing in these kinds of funds is especially important *until you have saved up enough to invest in individual stocks* that you can take the time to actively research, monitor, and follow on a regular basis. I've heard Cramer say more than once that if you have less than ten thousand dollars, you really have no reason to be investing in individual stocks. Use the index funds to offer you the diversity you need *until* you accumulate enough to invest in a diverse set of individual stocks. Said another way, Cramer emphasizes that you should not own individual stocks until you have a sufficient investment amount set aside to break away from the mutual funds/index funds most people start out with. Cramer believes (and now, so do I) that the best way to invest long-term is to buy a diversified portfolio of individual stocks; you have to do your own homework on each one of them—ideally you should spend one hour per week per stock—so that you know when it's time to buy more, when it's time to sell some, and maybe even when it's time to sell everything. That takes a commitment most people are not willing to make. But that is how you learn. That is how I learned.

The reality is that owning stocks can be very profitable, but it is really just one step in the wealth-building process that I follow today.

I can't possibly mention everything I learned from reading Cramer's books and hearing him on television, but I can say he, more than anyone else, has made me realize that *only I am responsible* for the final outcome of my financial security. He, more than any other author, changed the way I looked at money.

I had to take ownership, but I couldn't take ownership until I learned the lingo. My financial security, my wife's financial security is our responsibility—no one else's.

~~~~~~

In 2004 I read a book entitled, *Younger Next Year: Live Strong, Fit, and Sexy – Until You're 80 and Beyond* by Chris Crowley & Henry Lodge.

The essence of this book, which you should buy and read (there are men's and women's versions), is that *you should take charge of your body so that you can then take charge of your life*. Let me say that again. The essence of this book is that *you should take charge of your body so that you can then take charge of your life*.

The book covers everything from aging, exercise, the heart, and pain, to strength training and nutrition, and it goes into great detail on each topic (perhaps too much detail at times, but I still found it interesting and educational). I like that they ended the book with these simple rules listed in the appendix:

1. Exercise six days a week for the rest of your life.

2. Do serious aerobic exercise four days a week for the rest of your life.

3. Do serious strength training, with weights, two days a week for the rest of your life.

4. Spend less than you make.

5. Quit eating crap.

6. Care.

7. Connect and Commit.

So read this book—spend time in the sections that interest you and at least skim in some detail the rest. I do have a couple of friends who thought the book went into too much detail in some areas (that is why I say you may have to skim a few chapters).

Item 4, *Spend Less Than You Make*, is what sinks so many people when it comes to their finances. I hope you will be different and I hope you will learn to spend less than you make from now on. But my point for including this book is that you owe it to yourself to know and commit to the fact that you *can age in good health*. This book helps you to understand how to age in good health. I don't know about you, but I want to live a long and healthy life and I plan to have multiple streams of income in place to fund what I hope will be many years of financial security. More importantly, I want to be very active for the rest of my life—one of those active adult types, not one of those retirees who sits in their recliner every day all day—and I personally have a lot of things left on my bucket list left to do. I want to be active so I can travel and actually play with my grandchildren, not just sit in a recliner and watch them play.

Much like I believe in taking ownership of my finances, I am also trying to take ownership of my own health as best I am able. I know everything is not in my control—my mother died early of Alzheimer's—but I can still work to control what I can.

This book helped me to not only change the way I looked at money, it also made me look differently about how fit I can be for the rest of my life if I take control and follow their seven simple steps outlined above.

~~~~~~

I've read several of Robert Kiyosaki's books, including:

> *Rich Dad, Poor Dad*

> *Rich Dad's Cashflow Quadrant: Rich Dad's Guide to Financial Freedom*

> *Rich Dad's Guide to Investing*

You may want to do as I did and make real estate part of your diversified portfolio. Don't believe all of those late-night television shows that make you think you should use no money down and leverage and flip yourself to millions. Go at it slowly and wisely and find a knowledgeable realtor that you can work with to help guide you. I talk more about our approach to real estate in Step 8.

Kiyosaki helped me to change the way I looked at money and he helped me to understand the basics of how to invest in real estate, how to use entities to protect my family, and how to use real estate as another way to diversify our assets.

~~~~~~

You absolutely can't go wrong reading anything written by Dave Ramsey. Take for instance his book, *The Total Money Makeover: Classic Edition: A Proven Plan for Financial Fitness.*

He teaches, through first-hand experience, how to get out of debt, regain control of your finances, and build wealth. His book is not a get-rich-quick book. He has developed a roadmap that is proven and he will guide you through how to develop your own roadmap to regaining control of your finances.

He starts off his book by explaining his *Total Money Makeover Challenge*, and then walks you through what most people go through: denial (or, "I'm not that bad off"), debt and money myths so many us have been taught, how to save that first $1000, building an emergency fund, college funding, maximizing retirement savings, and so much more.

Read it, and most importantly, do the worksheets and develop your own roadmap to financial security.

Ramsey helped me to change the way I looked at money. He helped me to be honest about several money myths I had been raised on and believed to be true.

~~~~~~

All of my formal education was in electrical engineering, so it was primarily through my informal or personal reading of so many of these authors' books that I have learned to let my money work *for me* rather than me working for money. That is a huge point I am trying to make in this book. Change the way you look at money. Let your money work for you! Diversify! If you don't understand something, then *learn it*, don't fear it.

I recommend you read everything you can to learn enough to understand and be able to make most of your own financial decisions.

I used a broker and trusted him to make decisions for me for a couple of years … big mistake. He pushed mutual funds with front loads and only called when he was pushing new funds to try to get me to switch to (after all, he got his fees upfront when he pushed front-load funds whether I made money or not). I was not a big enough client to really be on his radar, so he did not watch my funds closely. I completely followed the advice and switched to the latest-greatest new fund the broker told me I should buy, but he made his commission and I lost money each year I followed his direction.

I manage my own portfolio now with the help of advisors, and of course I talk to my accountant for tax-related decisions on a regular basis. I still read and do a good deal of my research; you should too.

~~~~~~

My point in this Step 2, *Change the Way You Look at Money*, has been to get you to read a *diverse set of books* that will help you understand key concepts that have helped me learn to save, invest, and diversify. The books above and many others I have read have helped me to change the way I looked at money and investing. You too should learn about:

- Understanding *how* to invest.

- The power of compound interest.

- The need to diversify your investments.

- The need to get help, but make your own educated decisions.

- Establishing and maintaining an emergency fund.

- Understanding how to read a prospectus.

- How to understand and create your own multiple streams of income.

- How to protect your assets.

We will talk about these topics, and more, throughout the remainder of this book.

Saying you want to be wealthy or achieve financial security

isn't good enough. You need to change the way you look at money, and that partly means learning about finances and taking ownership of your own financial security. But it also means having a plan and executing against that plan.

Action Steps For You

1. The first thing you need to do is be honest about your knowledge about investing. Are you afraid of money and investing? Do you understand investing? Do you agree that *only you* are responsible for your financial security and no one else is or even should be?

2. Finish *this* book and learn a little from my experiences.

3. Decide *now* to start increasing your knowledge about investing options and make a plan to always be learning more and more about investing. Read the books I wrote about in this chapter to increase your understanding and awareness about your investment options.

4. Develop your own list of books to read. Turn off the television and dedicate time to learning so you can get to the point where you are not afraid of money, you are able to ask the right questions when you talk to your advisors, and you are educated enough to make the decisions yourself through your own research and homework with the guidance of advisors. I have become an avid reader about investing and business, and it was really through my reading that I started to change the way I looked at money and investing.

5. Always save *while you are learning* about money and investing.

STEP 3: RECOGNIZE THAT YOU CANNOT LEARN EVERYTHING

In Step 2, I focused on learning, including learning *from* others. But you can never learn enough to go it alone. There will always be a need for experts to advise you.

One lesson I accepted early on is that no matter how much I learned, I would never be able to know it all and I would always need to rely on the advice of others. In the meantime, I put my energy into learning enough to be able to get by with the input of others. When it comes to investing, I also realized early on that I would *always* be in the learning mode, since the world of investing is ever-changing.

Let me tell you a little more about my story and how learning has been a never-ending source of joy for me.

I spent most of my years in the Air Force working on the systems acquisition side, where I used my Bachelor's and Master's degrees in electrical engineering to work on and oversee multiple engineering projects. I was not satisfied to simply do my job and go home. I learned everything I could about the systems acquisition process—contracts, finance, specifications, statements of work, etc.—so that I could deliver the best programs to our airmen and service partners and get the best bang for the taxpayers' buck. I took my job seriously, and I took my on-the-job education seriously, too. I treated every day as continuing education—as a chance to learn something new.

> *We have an innate desire to endlessly learn, grow, and develop. We want to become more than what we already are. Once we yield to this inclination for continuous and never-ending improvement, we lead a life of endless accomplishments and satisfaction.*
> *— Chuck Gallozzi*

One thing that stood out to me in the Air Force systems acquisition field was that there was so much to learn, and there was no way I could ever learn it all. I decided to focus on understanding everything I could about the *big picture* of systems acquisition — that is, the process (or basic, repeatable steps, from beginning to end) of turning a concept or an idea into a fielded system. When it came to the details of things like finance or contracts or some technical aspect I did not know, I made sure I knew who the experts where in those areas and I relied on their input and advice.

The key for me was to always look at the big picture and then decide in advance where I needed input. I also knew that I needed to build relationships with those experts over time so I could go to them when I needed their help.

Do the same thing: look at the big picture of whatever problem you are trying to solve and determine where you need expert advice. Then, start building those relationships early so they are there when you need them and you do not have to develop those relationships *while* you are in the middle of solving a problem. Let those experts and advisors know how you can help them — it is a two-way street.

Good leaders know themselves — their strengths and weaknesses — and they rely on other people who complement those capabilities and shortcomings. You can spend all of your time trying to reinvent the wheel, or you can learn enough to work with and oversee others who specialize in things you do not know, and together you can accomplish far more than you ever could alone. Let the experts in their fields (e.g., accountants, lawyers, financial planners, tax specialists) do their jobs and do not try to do it all yourself!

> *The way of a fool is right in his own eyes, but he that hearkeneth unto counsel is wise.* — *Proverbs 12:15 (KJV)*

I focus on being really good at what I do, but I know I am a big-picture person, and I outsource or delegate everything else. I continue to learn, and I look ahead to understand the changing landscape, but I hand off everything I do not want to do, do not like to do, or am just not good at. After many years in this business, I know myself pretty well—I know what I am good at and I know what I am not good at.

> *He who knows others is learned.*
> *He who knows himself is wise.* — *Lao Tse c.604-531 BC*

~~~~~

What worked for me can work for you! While I want to know enough to be able to make educated decisions, I also know that I can never become fully knowledgeable about everything my advisors have to offer. That is *why* we have advisors and mentors. No one expects you to know everything or to have to learn everything. Become an expert at something and surround yourself with experts you can rely on when you need help.

I have learned enough about finance, contracts, legal matters, and taxes to get by, but I am not an expert in any of those. So I rely heavily on the input of my team of advisors and experts.

To be honest, I don't *want* to be an expert in any of those things. But I also don't want others making decisions that I need to be making, so I learned enough over the years to be able to make those educated decisions once I've met with my team and gone over their advice and options.

Whatever path you choose, you are probably going to need the expertise of those same types of advisors.

I also urge you to surround yourself with some well-chosen *mentors* that have been successful and are willing to guide you as you go about executing your chosen path.

For example, if you decide to start a business, then by all means meet with and talk to people who have started their own business. You can save yourself a lot of grief by learning from mentors who have already struggled through it. It also helps to have mentors you can call on when you are confronted with a challenge.

If you want to look into getting medical benefits for your employees, then don't go it alone. Talk to other business owners about their lessons learned in comparing benefit options. What types of plans did they consider? Who did they go to when they needed to get quotes? Why did they go the route they did?

If you are setting up a retirement plan for your employees, then again, talk to others who have set up retirement plans. Ask them what companies they considered, what options they considered, and what option they decided on. Ask them why they decided upon that option.

For almost anything you want to do in life, you will find that you can get ahead faster if you recognize that you do not have to go it alone; you do not have to learn everything.

Yes, accountants, lawyers, financial planners, tax specialists, and the like can be expensive advisors. But in the long run, you don't know what they know and you will end up far ahead by paying for their advice.

Having mentors whom you meet with regularly will also help you get ahead faster and save you money as well.

In the book *The Power of Focus* that I discussed in Step 2, the authors dedicate an entire chapter on *Building Excellent Relationships*.

They advise you to start now to build a team of trusted advisors and mentors before you *need* them. Don't wait until you need their help or are in the middle of a crisis. Those same advisors may actually help you *avoid* a crisis before it happens.

They authors talk about *Making Yourself Bulletproof* by building a fortress around you—by building *Your Unique Total Support System* that *could* include experts, mentors, and advisors. They advise you to consider:

- The Family Unit
- Specific (to your needs) Mentors and Coaches
- Health and Fitness Team
- Business Support Team (Interior – e.g., Administrative Staff, Sales, and Management Team)
- Business Support Team (Exterior – e.g., banker, lawyer, suppliers)
- Spiritual Adviser

While I did not list every element the authors talk about, you should be able to get the idea that you do not need to go it alone, and you do not *want* to go it alone.

Think about your home life and your work life and then decide where you need help. Read *The Power of Focus* on *Building Excellent Relationships* for a more detailed overview of how you can build a fortress around you.

I can't emphasize enough the importance of building the fortress and your relationship with mentors, advisors and experts over time. It takes work to build this team, but having them available when you need them will help prevent making rash, uneducated decisions while in the middle of a crisis or while solving a difficult problem.

Action Steps For You

1. Be honest with yourself about what you know and what you need to know.

2. Recognize that you can't learn everything and it is okay to need a team to help you out. Pick and chose what you need to get smarter on and then get busy learning as I did.

3. Find a mentor or set of mentors to guide you. Who is it that you know that has been successful in an area you want to excel at? Make it a point to meet them. Be bold enough to ask for some of their time.

4. Build a team of experts around you: accountant, tax advisor, real estate agent/advisor, lawyer, banker, etc. Start building your own *fortress* of support today.

5. Meet with your team on a regular basis, but respect their time. Be prepared and make the best use of their valuable time.

6. Treat every day as a chance for continuing education to stretch you, acquire more skills and learn something new. At the end of every day, ask yourself:

    What did I learn today?

    What did I stretch myself on today?

    What will I stretch myself on tomorrow?

7. Start every project with the *big picture* in mind. What do you know about the project? What do you not know enough about and will need an expert advisor or mentor to help you with? Break the big picture into smaller pieces and tackle them one at a time so the project will not seem so overwhelming. Treat your learning the same way. Look at the big picture as you decide what you need to learn in

general, and then what order you need to learn things in. If you don't start with the big picture and the basics and then drill down from there, you will feel overwhelmed, thinking you can never learn enough about investing — as I did at the beginning.

STEP 4: MAKE A COMMITMENT TO NEVER STOP SAVING AND INVESTING

Much like I have made a commitment to always be learning, I have made a commitment to always be saving and to always be investing. That's easy to say and easy to *commit to*, but sticking to that commitment and actually following through—every week…every month…every year—was hard work; it *is* hard work, and we were not always successful. But now we do things almost by instinct. You can too if you are disciplined.

Unless you are lucky enough to receive a large inheritance, you'll need to make the same kind of commitment and navigate your own route to financial security. But while Bill Gates-like wealth may be elusive for most, securing your financial security is definitely within reach of those who start young and develop the right habits. Anyone, at any age, can develop the *habits* that increase wealth and decrease debt. That's what this book is really about: the habits and traits we developed over the years that have worked for us.

For most people, early in life you need to decide if you want *stuff* or if you want money that will help you achieve financial security. I don't know too many younger people who choose to regularly focus on saving for financial security, because they (like I did) believe financial security is just too far off to worry about. Most young people are trying hard to just get by and pay their monthly bills. They want more things so they take out loans or put their purchases on their credit cards. They put the minimum down on their purchases and they are forever paying off their purchases and loans—loans that include interest, which could be going into their savings.

I hope you will be different. I hope you will accept the fact that only you are responsible for your financial security. Not the government. Not your boss. Not your advisor. Not your spouse alone, but you and your spouse together.

The truth is, unless you are lucky enough to be born into a rich family that will continue to support you, in order to achieve financial security, you will need to develop habits that I'll discuss throughout this book. The earlier you develop those habits, the easier it will be to enjoy financial security with the finances you hope to have.

People often look at the wealthy and wish they were also wealthy, but a lot of those same people, instead of focusing on how they could be making more money, will spend all of their energy making excuses about why they are not making enough money or never will. I hear these excuses all the time:

I can't save any money.

I won't be able to retire.

I don't make enough money.

Investing is too hard.

I don't know how to invest.

I've heard all these statements before, and many more. I used to make the same excuses. Most of us have negative stories we tell ourselves about money, and excuses for why we can't succeed financially, especially when a lot of the money advice we hear seems impossible to follow, impossible to understand, or just not applicable to us.

The commitment you can make is to put all of that *noise* behind you. If you tell yourself you can never understand investing so you don't bother learning, then you only have yourself to blame and you will always be depending upon someone else to make your investment decisions for you.

If you are living paycheck-to-paycheck or struggling to pay off debt, you might find this all just a little hard to swallow and implement, and in fact, it may seem impossible. Also, if you have money to invest, but no idea where to start, the range of investing options can seem overwhelming. Inexperience and negative self-talk can paralyze you from even getting started. I know this too, because I used to say the same things to myself. I used to think I could never learn enough about investing to make my own financial decisions. I put in the time, and over time, I learned. That is exactly what you need to do too!

I can assure you, whatever your situation may be, if you can just start letting go of old excuses that enable bad habits and adopt a new, more positive money mindset, and take incremental minor steps, you will have made the first critical step in achieving financial security. Your first step may be to stop making excuses. But then you need to make a commitment to yourself and to your spouse, like we did.

So, what *are* some of the habits we *committed* to in order to achieve financial security?

1. We SAVED—we saved something, no matter how small; we saved small amounts, and over time, we grew the amount we saved.

2. We lived below our MEANS—and we still do.

3. We limited our use of CREDIT —and for many years now we only use a credit card if we have the cash to pay it off as soon as the monthly bill arrives.

4. We created a simple FINANCIAL PLAN—we still have a financial plan and we revisit where we are with our plan regularly.

5. We INVESTED—we learned to not just save, but to invest, and we diversified our investments.

6. We REBALANCED our investments — we do this annually and sometimes quarterly or semi-annually.

Let's look at some of these habits in detail.

1. WE MADE A COMMITMENT TO SAVE

We SAVED — we saved something, no matter how small; we saved small amounts, and we grew the amount we saved over time.

This is really a first step if you plan to get ahead. You must commit to save something and be disciplined in your savings. For *most* people, there is almost always something you can give up to put toward your financial security.

We Spent Less Than We Earned

This is *savings 101*, but old advice can be good advice. Every paycheck, you must spend less than you earn. To get started, open a savings account or money market account purely for separating and keeping this extra money and add to it regularly, but don't tap into this separate account for normal expenses. This account should be different from your everyday account that you use to pay your bills from, and it should preferably be one that has a higher interest rate than your usual savings account.

The habit of saving really does require a lot of self-discipline. Spend time working to eliminate those bad habits that take away your self-discipline and your ability to save. Focus on what you can *accomplish* by saving rather than *buying more and more stuff* you don't need anyway.

Setting up that separate account is one of the many ways in which you can make your money work for you. Your initial deposit of money grows as you make additional deposits. Learn the different types of accounts and decide which one works for you.

We Lived on One Income for Many Years and We Still Saved

Many families are dual-income families and they find themselves leveraged so much that they need both paychecks just to pay the bills each month. We lived on one paycheck for the majority of our working lives, and so can you. It is a choice. Many people will disagree and say they absolutely need both paychecks. In some cases that is true. But in a lot of situations it all comes down to the choices we make about what things we need in our lives; often, we put those things at a higher priority than saving to get ahead. Never put yourself in a situation where you absolutely need both incomes and can't afford for one of you to be out of work. But more importantly, if you are a dual-income family, live on one salary and invest the other salary to help you achieve your financial goals earlier than most people are able to.

No matter how big your income is, never depend on the entire income. It seems that no matter how much a person makes, they always want more stuff — a bigger house, a second house, a newer car, another newer car. Before long you've leveraged yourself so much that you cannot get by without that entire salary (or both salaries). If you then find yourself out of work or taking a pay cut and you have not put aside emergency funds (Step 6), you will be in a real financial bind.

I knew a coworker who was earning $250,000 a year and he insisted he needed his entire salary just to get by. He was always complaining that he was strapped and could not afford to do anything fun. But he also had a house much bigger than he would ever truly need, and he traded in his new cars every few years, taking out five-, sox-, and seven-year loans each time to pay for them.

I don't even want to think about the interest he is paying on the car loans each month. It's no wonder he can't save! No wonder he does not have enough money to travel overseas as he is always talking about doing *someday when he can save the money*.

Some (including our children) might say that we did without a lot of things while living on one income, but it was a personal choice that Becky and I agreed to and it worked for us. It allowed Becky to focus more time with the children as they grew up. We may have had less stuff — smaller houses, older cars, etc. — and we lived on a military paycheck for many years, but we got by just fine.

We Did Not Start Saving Early; You Should Learn from Us and Start Now, Regardless of Your Age

The sooner you put your money to work, the more time it has to grow. Earning a paycheck, whether you are self-employed or work for a company, means you have the opportunity to contribute to a retirement account, which you should do. If you're fortunate enough to get a job with a company that offers a matching contribution to their retirement plan, you need to make it a priority to enroll in the plan as soon as you become eligible. We made sure our 401(k) contributions at least met the point where we could max out the company matching. If you don't take advantage of company matching, you are throwing away money.

As an example of why you should start investing early, if you made a one-time investment of $10,000 and left it to grow for forty years, assuming an average return per year of 8 percent, you would end up with about $217,000. Whereas, if you waited ten years and invested twice as much, $20,000, you would *only* end up with just over $200,000. Let *time* be your friend and start saving early in your life.

It is important to have your money invested for a long time. Let the basics of *time value of money* and compound interest work for you rather than trying to play catch-up with your savings later in life. The longer your money is invested, the more opportunity there will be for your growth to compound and your ups to far outweigh your downs. The longer you wait to start saving, you will find that you have to put far *more* away each month to catch up, as illustrated in the previous paragraph example.

We Use Retirement Accounts to Help Us Avoid Taxes

Take some time to read up on tax-advantaged retirement accounts, like 401(k), 403(b), traditional or Roth IRAs, and Simplified Employee Pension (SEP) Plans. When you invest in these kinds of accounts, you can avoid paying taxes on market growth (capital gains), which really makes a big difference in how much you can accumulate over your lifetime. Use every tax-advantaged approach to saving available to you.

We Automated Our Savings

You can be your own worst enemy when it comes to your financial success. So do everything you can to take yourself out of the equation on the simple things. For example, the best way to protect yourself from yourself is to automate your savings and your retirement deductions. That means setting up recurring transfers on a regular basis from your checking account to your savings and investment accounts. Set up auto deduction from your paycheck to your employer-sponsored retirement plan; this can be done easily.

Most people tend to want to buy more stuff. We are wired that way! When you automate your savings you no longer *see* the money every month so you will be less likely to spend it. Even if it is only a small amount that you automate at first, those steady investments can make a big difference over time. Automate whatever you can whenever you can; just be careful to avoid dipping into your account and try to increase the amount you save over time.

Not only should you start investing as *early* as possible, you should also contribute as *much* as possible to your investments. Consider this example: if you invest $10,000 today and add $500 per month versus $250 per month for forty years, assuming an 8 percent return, you will have over $1 million more saved by investing the extra $250 per month.

> *$10,000 invested today; add $250 per month for forty years at 8 percent = over $1.8 million.*

> *$10,000 invested today; add $500 per month for forty years at 8 percent = over $3 million.*

Many books today recommend that most of us need to be investing 10-15 or even 20 percent of our annual income in order to reach our long-term savings goals. But they recommend that amount because most of us wait too long to focus on financial security or retirement needs.

Do your own calculations! Go online and search on *Investment Calculator* and see for yourself (there are a lot of calculator sites to choose from).

Plug in several combinations of numbers and interest rates and see what small incremental changes over the long term can mean to your retirement account.

2. WE MADE A COMMITMENT TO ALWAYS LIVE BELOW OUR MEANS

We have always lived below our *means* – we still do, and always will.

We make hard choices. We always ask ourselves if we need to spend the money now.

Sure, there are a lot of *things* we would love to own. But we have learned to put our wants and our egos in check and we sleep so much better knowing that we are not living beyond our means.

If you can't afford that expensive car or that boat, then get rid of it. Don't stretch yourself beyond your earnings by buying things just to keep up with others.

Part of living below your means is learning to avoid temptation. Today, we are inundated with ads through the television, the Internet, magazines, you name it — there are ads everywhere trying to divert our attention to *want* something. So we buy it. Try to just never buy the moment you see something. Force yourself to let some time go by and often you will realize you really don't need that item so bad after all.

We decided a long time ago not to be comparing ourselves or what we have to others or what they have. It is all too easy to listen to the ads that make you feel like you must keep up with those around you — or even get ahead of those around you. Don't fall into that trap.

Key to the point I'm making about living below your means is that life is about choices, and the choices you make with every dollar you spend will determine whether you can live below your means or live on credit and possibly never achieve financial security.

3. WE MADE A COMMITMENT TO USE CREDIT CARDS RESPONSIBLY

We have always limited our use of credit, and for many years now we only use a credit card if we have the cash to pay it off as soon as the monthly bill arrives. If you constantly max out your credit card and are not saving, you are going to find it hard to become financially secure at any stage in your life.

I'm pretty sure the credit-card companies hate us, because we don't pay monthly credit-card fees and we never pay monthly interest payments. We pay the credit card off as soon as the monthly bill is due.

I am not saying you should never use credit cards; I am saying you should learn to use your credit cards responsibly.

Limit the number of credit cards you own. Pay off the bill each month so you never pay interest. Use credit cards that don't require an annual fee. If you have multiple credit cards, pay off the balance of the credit cards with the highest interest rates and highest fees and then close those accounts.

But there are ways to use the credit card to your advantage — ways to use your credit cards responsibly.

A lot of credit cards allow you to earn *rewards* in the form of points that can be turned into cash, gift certificates, or even travel. We have cut thousands off of our travel budget by using the rewards points we accumulated over the years.

You can build up your credit if you use your card responsibly and pay your bill on time each month. Having that strong credit will pay off in the long run too, because when you have strong credit you can get lower interest rates on larger purchases like your home. A savings of a few percentage points on a fifteen-, twenty-, or thirty-year loan can be significant. Mortgage companies want to see that you have a strong track record of paying your bill on time each month over a period of time. A credit card is one way to build up that strong credit reputation.

Some people will argue that you should never use credit cards; I argue you should limit the number of credit cards you have and you should use your credit cards responsibly. You will come out ahead financially in the long run.

4. WE MADE A COMMITMENT TO HAVE A FINANCIAL PLAN AND LIVE TO OUR FINANCIAL PLAN

We created a simple financial plan and we still have a financial plan that we recheck regularly to assess where we are against that plan. A plan is meant to be monitored and your progress assessed against it; it should not become what I call "shelf-ware" (a plan that is created and read and then shelved never to be looked at again).

You can have a formal financial plan (or budget) or a less formal financial plan, but the key is to have a plan that you and your spouse agree to and you stick to. Also key to your financial plan is to set savings goals and to have an emergency fund that you never touch unless you have a real emergency.

You have plenty of resources available to help you create a financial plan, and you can download templates easily through a simple web search. For example, you can search on *free personal financial templates* and you can easily find sample financial plan formats or templates with guidelines to tailor to your needs.

With templates and guidelines readily available online, the point I want to make is that you *need* a financial plan and you and your spouse need to work together to put the plan in place. Then you need to work together to *follow* your plan.

Many people choose to avoid having a financial plan or just turn over their finances to an advisor. I personally think there are many things you can do yourself, or do with the help and input of an advisor, if you would just put fear behind you and take the time to learn and do some of these things yourself.

Financial plans you'll see online or advisors you work with will all ask you some common questions that only you can answer or decide on.

They always ask you some basic questions that require some soul-searching and discussion between you and your spouse. For example, they will always ask you what your goals are.

So Set Some Goals

You simply cannot put together a realistic financial plan if you don't know where your finances stand today. You also need to know where you want to be financially before you can set a path to get you to your goals. In the short-term you might be to pay off your credit cards. Middle-term goals might be to pay off your house in fifteen years instead of thirty years or save enough to pay for your children's college education. Longer-term might be to reach a financial target to allow you to retire at the age of your choice. You can have multiple short-, mid-, and long-term goals. We have always had a mix of the three. We don't wing it and you shouldn't either. Our goals are specific and measurable. Your goals will also need to be specific and measurable.

Write those goals down and assign a dollar amount and a target date to each goal. Regularly look at these goals and make sure you are working toward them—hold each other accountable.

As you go about putting your plan together, you need to have a good understanding of where you stand now financially. Start by calculating your net worth. Subtract your debts (liabilities like mortgage loan or credit-card balances) from the total value of what you own (include assets like your retirement and bank account totals).

Next, calculate what you can *reasonably* save each pay period, if anything, after you've covered expenses (include both fixed expenses, like rent or electric bills, and discretionary expenses, like eating out).

If you have a negative net worth or are in a negative monthly cash-flow situation, then all the more reason to do some financial planning. I've said it before: too much debt will only hurt your chances of achieving your financial goals. Look closely at every expense and start making your own hard choices about what you need and what you can live without. For most people, it will take serious financial planning and the conviction to follow your plan to get into a positive cash-flow situation and reach your financial targets.

As you set your goals for your financial plan, you need to make sure you have protected yourself for an unexpected illness, a job loss, and the inevitable market downturn. Make sure you have several months (six perhaps) of living expenses and make sure you have the right insurances in place. Don't do what a lot of people do and make yourself insurance poor — pay for insurance you need! Don't over-insure yourself and overpay for protection, but also don't under-insure yourself or you may find yourself needing funds to cover the gap. Your insurance protection should include adequate auto, renters or homeowners, health, disability, and life insurance, at a minimum. I talk in detail about *protecting your assets* in Step 9.

Some people rely on their home equity line of credit as their emergency fund, but that has the downside of putting you in more debt in emergency or crisis situations. Save until you get your emergency fund in place.

Take a close look at your taxes and make sure you maximize your deductions; if you are not sure how to do this then you need to talk to an accountant. Chances are your certified accountant will essentially pay for herself with the advice she offers in reducing your taxes.

Each of your goals will likely require a different investment strategy because of differences in time horizon and risk tolerance. You can help yourself if you set up automatic monthly contributions, choose low-cost investments, and maximize savings in tax-advantaged accounts like 401(k)s,

IRAs, SEPs and 529 college savings plans.

STRETCH! I encourage you to stretch yourself as you put your plan together. I find that many people put unrealistic goals in place, but at the same time, they do not put challenging goals in place. So set goals that will stretch you.

As I said, there is a lot you can do yourself to prepare your own financial plan, but if you find this all confusing, you should consider talking to a financial advisor. It is just that important to have a financial plan in place that you and your spouse agree to and can work together to meet.

Sometimes you have to spend money to make money, and you may have to spend money to put together a really good financial plan. So building a team around you that includes an experienced financial advisor, accountant, and, in certain complex cases, an estate planner is exactly what you need. The more complicated your estate is, the more likely you will need help in creating your financial plan.

For a lot of people, a financial plan you can download from the web will at least get you a great start until you need and can afford certified experts. I have personally found that I need the experts' input as our situation has grown more complicated. Yes, hiring and working with those experts will cost you, and you can still do some do-it-yourself planning, but their objectivity, expertise, personalized guidance, and ongoing monitoring can be well worth it—and help you sleep better at night.

5. WE MADE A COMMITMENT TO ALWAYS BE INVESTING

We INVESTED—we learned to not just save, but we learned to invest, and we diversified our investments to protect ourselves in case one investment area did not do as well as we expected. The old saying, "Never put all your eggs in one basket!" *is* very much applicable to your financial security.

Just Start Investing!

You really have three basic decisions to make: how much money to invest, how often you want to invest it, and how you want your asset allocation to look between cash, stocks, bonds, and the like. It's alright if you don't have a lot of money to invest right away; just decide to commit to get started.

Like with your savings plan we discussed, start investing a few bucks on a regular basis, but if you are able to invest more, then by all means do so. Also, once you start investing, don't stop every time the stock market has its ups and downs. Think *long-term*.

We Bought Mutual Funds First before Buying Individual Stocks.

When you own a mutual fund, you own the securities (stocks, bonds, cash) within the fund. With mutual funds, you are pooling your money with other investors and diversifying your investment. I don't recommend anyone start by putting their initial investment dollars into one stock or even a couple of stocks. You really want to always be diversified, so start with a diversified mutual fund or funds and as you grow your assets you will be able to start buying individual equities.

Make Sure You Don't Overpay in Fees!

Many mutual funds have a one-time sales charge (a.k.a. *load*) of up to 5 percent and an annual expense ratio of 1 to 2 percent if they are actively managed. A few percentage points may not seem like a lot to pay at first, over the long run it can amount to quite a bit. Learn enough to manage your own portfolio. Choose no-load funds whenever possible to help minimize cost and maximize your savings potential.

Eventually We Started Investing in Stocks

A lot of people go through life and never invest in individual stocks, but once we grew investments to greater than $50,000 we decided it was time to start diversifying into stocks we liked and had done our homework on. We eased out of mutual funds and into mostly stocks over time. But we diversified our stock investments. Remember, we had diversified through our mutual fund selections, so we did not want to put all of our assets into one or more stocks and be at risk of losing everything. We diversified into different stocks assets keeping an eye on the market and the performance of the stocks we owned.

Some people buy stocks and hold them forever. While I buy for the long term, I do not advocate the "buy and hold forever" approach. You need to monitor the performance of the stock to make sure it makes sense to continue to own it.

Also, if one stock does really well, you may become overly invested in that stock and no longer diversified or balanced enough. Always monitor, rebalance, and diversify as needed.

We Diversify Our Investments

More on this in Step 8, but we diversified our risk by buying across a variety of investments, from stocks, mutual funds, ETFs and bonds, to real estate, etc. A diversified portfolio means that you can potentially take advantage of multiple sources of growth and protect yourself from financial ruin if one of your investments goes bad.

Eventually We Tried Some Risky Investing

I am a risk taker. So once we had saved well over $100,000 I decided to try my hands at some of the more risky investments. Investors can make big money in these stocks by getting in before the crowd. I went small because I realize you can also *lose* a lot of money in those risky investments. I was not about to risk too much, but I have gradually gotten to the point where at times I invest up to 10% annually into risky companies. Some will argue that is too much to risk. You have to decide what you can invest and still sleep at night — and what you can afford to lose, because with these stocks you can lose all of your principal if the company tanks!

I looked into *game-breaker* stocks (a company that is potentially going to change the landscape of an industry, as Apple or Wal-Mart did in their respective sectors), *inflection-point* stocks (companies that have a broken business model that's on the mend but have yet to be recognized by the market), *stealth stocks* (companies that are often names unknown to the general public but can be hugely profitable investments especially when they have catalysts to boost their share prices).

So, Think Long Term

The quicker you start investing, the better. If you begin investing in your twenties or thirties, you will be able to take advantage of compounding interest and put yourself in a significantly better position than most people.

We Stayed in the Market

Many people, after experiencing steep losses during market downturns, may be quick to avoid equities altogether. But over time, stocks have historically provided the highest consistent returns of most investments.

Many people will operate out of fear and let their emotions drive their decisions, and they sell everything when the market drops. Selling low only assures you lose money and then you have to decide when to get back into the market. It's always easy to sell and get out of the market, but where will you invest if you do not invest at least some of your assets in equities? You sure can't leave your money in cash and hope that inflation does not eat away at your savings — it will!

Trust, but Verify

Don't buy stocks because your friends recommended it or because you read an article online where some analyst was touting a stock. Do your own homework!

We Were Not Overly Aggressive

We balanced our level of risk in equities but also in how much we wanted to put into the market. We diversified within the stock market but we invested outside the stock market (Step 8) to lessen our risks and exposure to equities.

Don't Chase Past Performance

Never buy a stock because of its past performance alone. What matters is how the company will perform going forward!

6. WE MADE A COMMITMENT TO REEVALUATE OUR FINANCIAL PLAN AND REBALANCE AND ADJUST AS NECESSARY

We REBALANCED our investments — we do this annually and sometimes quarterly or semi-annually.

Since different asset classes grow at different rates and some grow much faster than others over a given timeframe, you will need to rebalance your portfolio on a regular basis.

For example, if you started out this year with a balanced portfolio of 75 percent stocks and 25 percent bonds, a surge in stocks may cause you to have a larger percentage of your portfolio in stocks and a smaller percentage in bonds if you haven't rebalanced yet.

You may need to sell positions that have gotten too large and reinvest the proceeds in other positions that might help reduce risk and capitalize on other opportunities in your portfolio.

Action Steps For You

1. Remember I said the first commitment you can make is to put all of the internal *noise* behind you and just figure out and commit to a financial plan that works for you — quit telling yourself you have plenty of time left to worry about financial security.

   - Quit telling yourself you don't understand investing.

   - Quit telling yourself you don't make enough money.

   - Quit telling yourself you can't save.

2. Make your own list of commitments and then stick to those commitments. Act on those commitments.

   - Commit to save something every paycheck.

   - Commit to live below your means.

   - Commit to minimize credit.

   - Commit to having a financial plan.

   - Commit to invest.

   - Commit to rebalance.

STEP 5: DEAL WITH YOUR DEBT

I dealt with my debt. Here are some simple steps to deal with your debt.

1. Assess your debt situation.

2. Commit to putting together a plan to eliminate your debt.

3. Act now to eliminate your debt.

4. Stop the bleeding!

5. Consider the Ladder Method to debt reduction.

6. Consider the Snowball Method to debt reduction.

7. Consider counseling.

8. Never carry credit-card balances.

9. Contact your creditors about your situation and see if they will work with you.

10. Resist debt-consolidation programs.

Let's look at these one by one.

1. Assess Your Debt Situation

Take a look at your debt. How bad is it? Are you living paycheck to paycheck? Are you and your spouse both working and you have leveraged yourself so much that you need both incomes just to make ends meet? Do you and your spouse have a plan for what you would do if one of you lost your job? How would you pay those bills if one or more of those incomes suddenly ended?

2. Commit to Putting Together a Plan to Eliminate Your Debt

If you are married, have this conversation with your spouse. Assess your situation and then if you are in debt, agree and commit to eliminate debt and stay out of debt. You can't do this alone if you are married.

Don't even finish reading this book until you have assessed your situation and talked it over with your spouse and truly understand your debt situation — and have committed to figure out how to get out of debt.

Do you have a budget? Are you living within your budget? Chances are, if you have a budget and have gotten yourself into debt, you are really not serious about budgeting — so get serious about budgeting. There are plenty of tools online and plenty of books that have been written that can help you put together a budget. You need to have a budget and you need to live to your budget.

I know life gets in the way and there are unexpected costs that come up and throw off your budget, but that is never an excuse to not have a budget. It just means you and your spouse need to reassess your situation and adjust your budget to those new conditions.

3. Act Now to Eliminate Your Debt

I know this sounds simplistic, and I also know it usually is hard for everyone involved. But you have to start somewhere.

If you have debts to pay off, focus on those first BEFORE making investing your top priority. I know this book is, in many ways, about creating your financial security and investing in your future, but if you do not deal with your debt first, you may never achieve financial security.

There is no one magical answer to dealing with debt, so let's talk some options for you to consider.

4. Stop the Bleeding!

You stop the bleeding by not adding any more debt to your current debt situation, so you can eliminate the debt you already have.

So how can you eliminate your debt?

5. Consider the Ladder Method to Debt Reduction

This is a form of restructuring the way you pay your monthly debt payments. The ladder method is often described as follows:

- Determine what your total debt payment is today.

- List your debts from highest interest rate to lowest.

- Continue to make the same total payment amount, except pay *minimum* monthly payments on all debts except the *highest*-rate debt.

- Once the highest-rate debt is paid off, apply those new savings to the next-highest-rate debt.

- Keep following this approach until you are debt-free.

- When you can, apply an extra amount to the total payment to accelerate debt payoff.

Some financial advisors say that the ladder method will save you the most money over the long term, because you're getting those high interest rates out of the way first.

6. Consider the Snowball Method to Debt Reduction

Another common approach to paying off debt is called the snowball method. While the goal of eliminating debt is the same as in the ladder method, with this method, instead of using interest rates to determine which account to pay off first, you focus on the size of balances. You once again pay the minimum monthly payment required on each account, but you start putting the extra money on the account that has the lowest balance. Once it's paid off, shift the funds to the next one up and repeat until your debts are paid off.

If you are someone who needs to see results quickly, then the snowball method may be best for you because you will be paying off one of your debts sooner and reducing the total number of payments you are making monthly.

7. Consider Counseling

You may find that you need help in putting together a plan to eliminate your debt. Consider credit counseling through a group like the nonprofit organization National Foundation for Credit Counseling (NFCC), which offers low-cost financial counseling in offices across the country. Many of these types of nonprofit organizations provide services either free or at low cost to help clients get out of debt.

Your professional credit counselor can help you assess your debt situation and identify repayment options and money-management techniques that you may not be aware of or just did not think of. They will help you put a plan in place and often continue to meet with you to evaluate and assess your progress.

Another option: if you have or know of a good financial adviser, ask them if they can also help you work on a debt-elimination plan. You may find that they just want to mange your money and may not be interested or trained in debt-elimination planning, but some do work with their clients to create a debt-elimination plan and help monitor their progress.

These counseling methods add a layer of accountability that can help keep you focused on debt elimination.

Remember, should a personal financial hardship come to you and your family, you'll be able to weather the storm far better if you only have to worry about day-to-day living expenses rather than paying off debts.

8. Never Carry Credit-Card Balances

Once we got our debt paid off, we committed to never carrying credit-card debt again. Ever!

Yes, we often use our credit cards, but when the statement comes each month we immediately pay it off. We have not paid interest on a credit card in many years and plan to never again make an interest payment on a credit card.

A high-interest credit-card debt may be one of the biggest threats to your financial security. You may find yourself paying thousands in unnecessary fees and interest charges when you don't pay the full amount or develop the habit of only paying the minimum monthly payment. All of those fees and interest charges prevent you from saving to your potential. I know too many people who pay the minimum each month on their credit cards, and they can never seem to get ahead. If you ever want to be financially free, you have to eliminate the habit of carrying credit-card balances and paying minimums.

We live within our means and we basically only use our credit cards to earn rewards points that we can apply to our bucket-list items.

9. Contact Your Creditors about Your Situation and See If They Will Work With You

You may be surprised to realize that creditors are usually willing to work with you, especially if you are dealing with a financial hardship. Explain the situation you are in — be honest. Try to negotiate lower rates and repeat calls to your creditors periodically. If you explain that you are suddenly unemployed, are earning lower wages or any number of other possibilities out of your control, that simple phone call just might result in an offer from your creditor to waive your interest rate temporarily. If not, ask them how they can work with you to come up with a payment plan that is mutually beneficial. They want to be paid. But don't wait until your situation is out of control, or until you have missed several payments; talk to them as soon as possible.

10. Resist Debt-Consolidation Programs

I'm not a fan of debt-consolidation programs. They may be tempting, but they typically come with upfront and ongoing fees, and the application process can be time-consuming. Save yourself time and money by managing your debts yourself, or get counseling, but in most cases, avoid debt-consolidation programs altogether. People who just keep racking up debt and then consolidating those debts will always pay more out of pocket and in most cases never get ahead.

~~~~~

I've mentioned Dave Ramsey in a previous chapter. He has documented Six Reasons People Stay in Debt:

1. They want to keep up appearances.

2. They are unwilling to sacrifice.

3. They fear change.

4. They're addicted to "stuff."

5. They don't know how.

6. They're lazy.

If you are in debt for these same reasons then you need to admit it and work to change your behavior, or you will never get out of debt and *stay* out of debt.

Action Steps For You

1. Assess your debt situation and the real reasons you are in debt!

2. Commit to putting together a plan to eliminate your excuses or reasons and eliminate your debt.

3. Begin to act *now* to eliminate your debt.

4. First, stop the bleeding!

5. Consider the Ladder Method to reduce your debt.

6. Consider the Snowball Method to reduce your debt.

7. Consider counseling if you need help.

8. Never carry credit-card balances.

9. Contact your creditors one by one about your situation and see if they will work with you to reduce or eliminate your debt.

10. Resist debt-consolidation programs!

STEP 6: START AN EMERGENCY FUND

This will be a pretty short chapter and yet a very important one. I could sum up this chapter in one main point: aim to have a minimum of six to nine months of your typical living expenses saved in a safe, interest-bearing account.

Today, interest-bearing accounts don't offer much interest, but at least they are set up so that you can access the funds quickly if you really do have an emergency.

While I said you should set aside six months of funds, many experts say you should have around three to six months of expenses in your emergency fund. I realize everyone's situation is different and you may only see the need for three months of emergency funds—or you may want to be even more prepared and have nine to twelve months of expenses saved up. But whatever you decide, get started building up your emergency funds *now*, because life always has a way of throwing off your monthly financial and budget plans.

Medical problems arise. The dental visit where you just planned to have your teeth cleaned turns into the need to have a crown that is not fully covered by your dental plan (if you even have a dental plan). You may experience flooding like that which occurred in South Carolina this year and be one of the many people who never realized flooding was even possible where you live…so you don't have flood insurance. The list goes on and on. Life carries on whether you are financially prepared or not.

Today, more households than not are dual-income, with families living off both incomes and often spending it all each month while saving very little. If one income earner loses a job or has a health issue (or even worse, a disability preventing them from continuing to bring home a paycheck), the other income can't serve as a bailout, because you have gotten yourself into a position where you depend on *both* incomes just to meet your monthly needs.

If that happens, then you have stretched yourself too far. I see it every day: as families grow to two incomes or as they get raises, they tend to just spend or obligate the extra money each month instead of saving or investing or growing their emergency fund.

Some financial advisors say you should make *saving* the priority if you have no emergency fund (to prevent going into further debt if an unexpected expense arises) and I personally agree. No matter how hard you try to get ahead, life gets in the way and you need to grow your emergency fund. Put some emergency funds set aside *now* and gradually grow that emergency fund over time. This approach—slowly building an emergency fund while paying down your debt (as we discussed in Step 5)—may also be one of the best ways to change your *negative money habits* and retrain yourself to be more financially responsible.

Besides building your emergency fund, I know you may want to get started on your investing or allocate more money to your investing, but keep in mind that debt costs you money. So unless your investments are making more than your debt is costing you, it usually makes sense to pay off your debt as soon as you can. Look at it this way: if you have a credit card that is charging 23 percent interest, you would need to be investing the money and earning at least a 23 percent return or better in order to have an investment that is worth it. In the cases where it isn't, pay off your debt instead.

Consider these points to help get your emergency fund in order:

1. Get in the habit of saving money right now no matter how small, but increase the amount of your weekly or monthly savings over time to build up your emergency fund.

2. Spend less than you earn — always!

3. Build an emergency fund in an easy-to-access money-market or other interest-bearing account so you don't have to wait on or raid from your savings and investments when unexpected expenses come up.

4. Make it a point to save at least half of every pay raise you get. Early on, when I got raises we put the entire raise into savings and pretended like we did not get a raise; it was so much easier to save that way. Over time, once we had our emergency fund built up and had a reasonable savings, we then allowed ourselves to spend some of the raise.

5. If you file your annual taxes and get money back from the IRS, don't spend it; use the money to pay down debt and/or build up your emergency fund. Once your debt is under control and your emergency fund is adequate, then consider investing.

6. If you have an emergency and don't have some liquid cash saved up, you're likely to go into debt and then pay interest on that debt. Your goal should be to avoid debt!

7. Focus on paying down debt with the difference between your earning and your spending *while* you also build up your emergency fund.

8. Fund your emergency account by automatic payroll deduction and don't touch it. If you haven't already, set

up a separate account and then use the automatic payroll method so you never see the money.

9. Expect expenses like new tires, dentist's bills, home repairs, and home upkeep, even though they are not a part of your monthly expenses. If you haven't set aside the money for these kinds of expenses, you will find that the cost of these expenses is much greater when you have to incur debt to buy those items. Paying interest on a loan or charge on your credit card in addition to the real cost of the expense will just put your further behind.

10. When you do use your emergency funds — only for true emergencies — replace them as soon as possible so the account will have time to build back up before you may need it again.

11. People (including myself) get hit with major unplanned expenses. When these things happen — and they will, more often than you might think — not having a financial safety net can make the situation much worse.

Action Steps For You

1. Figure out *how much of an emergency fund you need* to have in place. Is it three months of income? Six months of income? Set that amount as a target and be relentless in working toward that amount.

2. Reread and consider the eleven points outlined above and determine how you can change your behavior to build up your emergency fund. This may take some time, but don't let that hold you back.

STEP 7: START A COMPANY. THEN START OTHER COMPANIES

I love what I do, and if you are willing to work hard, then you, too, can escape the 8-to-5 grind, create your own path, and start and grow your own business(es). Here is an in-depth look at my background and work experience. My hope is that by knowing more about my work, and about me, you will not only understand why I wrote this book and believe that I am qualified to write it, but you will also understand the experiences that ultimately shaped my business strategies.

It was those work experiences that shaped my ability and confidence to start my first company, RazoRealty LLC, a family-owned real estate investing company. The idea I had with RazoRealty was to diversify my investments by buying real estate. In particular, I wanted to use RazoRealty to buy very distressed single-family homes, gut them and rehab them, and then rent them out. While I can't say I was especially talented or knowledgeable about gutting and rehabbing houses, I must say I have learned a lot. My youngest son, Ryan, is involved in RazoRealty, and it has been a blast to work with him to rehab the houses and then rent them out. We have both learned a lot—about rehabbing, about each other, and about ourselves. How many people get to work side-by-side with their children? And today, I easily have over a million dollars in real estate and a steadily growing investment stream. And this is just one stream in my model. My idea and my plan was to diversify into multiple streams of income and not focus my energy on just one stream of income.

Today, in my sixties, I consult primarily as a business coach and mentor through my company The Unconventional Strategist. The company name says it all; I work with you, or with you and your executive team, to help strategize and think *unconventionally* about growing personally and professionally. I can help you map out a plan to start, grow, and even sell a company — if that is your goal. I provide business and management consulting services to companies of all sizes. My specialties and background include business startup and consulting, executive consulting/coaching, systems engineering, and systems integration.

Today, I have ownership in multiple businesses. You can own one or more companies, too, if that is what you choose to do. I admit, it takes hard work, and it takes time. It also requires putting together a strategy, which is just one of the things I can help you with through The Unconventional Strategist.

A Little Bit about My Background

I am able to consult today through The Unconventional Strategist because I have spent my working years doing the very things I mentor, advise, and consult others on. I didn't just decide one day to start a consulting company. I spent my working years mastering my chosen field so that I could mentor, advise, and consult on it.

I started my first company and got it up and running, and then I started (and partnered with others to start) other new companies that we continue to oversee and grow.

Let me tell you a little more about my background so you can better understand how I ended up with ownership in multiple companies and why I am qualified to mentor others.

My background includes twenty years in the Air Force as a systems acquisition expert followed by twenty-plus years as a government contractor, business owner, business consultant, and now author. After retiring from the Air Force, I served in executive management positions with annual revenues of up to $160 million, including Corporate Vice President at SAIC, President and COO of McClendon Corporation, and President at ICES, providing support to various U.S. government agencies.

When I look back over my early years in the Air Force, I never gave much thought to owning my own business, let alone owning more than one. Instead, I focused on doing the best I could in whatever job I had. When I became a contractor, I started to get the entrepreneurial bug and to think about owning my own business and setting my own agenda.

Here's a little more about how I made the leap from Air Force veteran to the owner (and in many cases, founder) of multiple companies:

After the Air Force, I joined SAIC (Science Applications International Corporation), a very entrepreneurial company. I loved SAIC because the managers I worked for were entrepreneurs. They had a "you kill it, you eat it" approach to business and were happy to reward employees who shared this spirit. In plain English, that means if you devise an idea for new business, market it, chase it, and eventually win that work, they will let you manage it and will reward your hard work.

My managers' attitude was, if you have an idea and it makes business sense, they would provide you with the support resources you need to be successful — and they did. I came up with the concepts/ideas, wrote white papers (also called concept papers), and submitted them to customers recommending ways to do things better, smarter, faster. My SAIC managers provided technical experts to review the white papers, and contracts and finance experts to review or write their sections, and we grew and grew as we chased more and more work.

Essentially, my managers empowered me; they provided expertise I did not have (in the form of other staff and other experts), and they rewarded me for the work that I created (killed)—they let me oversee (eat) the work. By the time I left SAIC, I was a corporate vice president and our last business unit had grown to a $160 million unit. I got the *entrepreneurial bug*!

I was recruited away from SAIC and became President of McClendon Corporation, a company with about 120 employees and annual revenue of about $18 million. The owners were thinking seriously about retirement, and they wanted to put others in charge, who could help grow their company. (The owners wanted to eventually sell the company, which they did, for about $66 million.)

Going to such a small company, after working at SAIC, which had many thousands of employees, was quite a change. But the McClendon Corporation owners had big goals and wanted to grow their company rapidly. We hired great employees, incentivized them, and provided them back-office support so they could focus on being great at their job—and the company grew and grew. Just a short fourteen months later, the company had over 220 employees and an annual revenue stream that had almost doubled.

Since I had worked in the government (Air Force) and as a contractor, I had a solid understanding of how the government side of business worked, and I had a solid understanding of how the contractor side of business worked. At McClendon, I learned a lot about working in the small-business world, and those lessons melded well with what I learned in the Air Force and at SAIC.

I got the *small-business bug*—big time! I knew I would enjoy operating in the small- and medium-business environment where bureaucracy was not the norm. I hate bureaucracy—it probably stems from my years in the Air Force, working classified programs where we were always understaffed and had tight deadlines to meet. Our daily mantra was to press on to get the mission done with as little bureaucracy as possible. The nice thing about the small-business world is that bureaucracy is not the norm; in fact, bureaucracy is typically pushed aside to enable performance.

I left McClendon Corporation after fourteen months and joined with two partners to grow the newly formed ICES (Intelligence Consulting Enterprise Solutions, Inc.), another government contracting company. Yes, there were just the three of us, but let it be noted that ICES is still a flourishing multimillion-dollar company, even as I write this book. Now I have another new stream of income—another company I own (or co-own with my two partners).

In summary, after leaving the Air Force, I went from a 40,000+ person company, where I had a nice big corner office with a nice title of corporate vice president, to a 120-employee company, with a modest corner office, to a three-person company, where we worked out of our homes. To some people—maybe to most people—it might appear that I moved backward in my career. In reality, my Air Force career and my subsequent contractor jobs shaped and prepared me to do what I do today—and I am doing what I love to do.

Mentoring and Consulting

Over the years, people often asked me how to network, to take an idea from the conception stage to an end product, to start a company, to grow a company, to get contracts, to strategize, and more. I was always hearing people say that they would love to start their own company, but they just did not know how to go about it. I began mentoring individuals in those skills and on many additional topics, like how to build rates to propose to the customer, to write a white paper, to respond to a request for proposals, to write proposals, and much more.

In other words, I was always mentoring and consulting and helping people to strategize (often for free). The most exciting thing is that I really loved mentoring and consulting and strategizing, so I decided it was time to get paid for my consulting work. I decided it was time to reshape my own strategy and my own vision, and to act on that vision.

My Business Concept and Vision

Several years ago I started working on a personal business concept, in which I would work with other entrepreneurs to start several new businesses to do different kinds of technical specialties, like systems engineering, security engineering, information technology (IT), network engineering, etc. I would also start a series of businesses to provide those companies the services and back-office support they need, so they could focus on being really great at their technical expertise. My thought was, much like at SAIC, if talented and entrepreneurial people could start their own companies but outsource all of the work they do not want to do, do not know how to do, or are not good at, then they could put all of their energy into their core (or specialty) skills where their passions lie. They could grow their company and be successful in their technical specialty (without the burden of learning the details of things they really did not need to learn or have the time to learn).

There were several elements to my original business concept. Some of those key elements, while rough, included:

- Start one company, grow it, incentivize someone to run it. Move on to start another company of my own, while serving on the board of directors of each startup company.

- Find entrepreneurs who have specific technical skills to sell and who want to start a company (but do not know how to start or run a company), and partner with them for some percentage ownership.

- Work with my companies to grow until they are recognized in an industry and have a strong record, and then target small-business set-aside prime contracts requiring their skills.

- Repeat the first three steps over and over each year.

- Start companies that provide all the back-office services (contracts, finance, budget, program controls, human resources, administration, etc.) that any small- or medium-size company needs to be successful. Encourage my technical companies to outsource all back-office functions, so the entrepreneurs of the technical companies could then focus on their technical specialties and grow the company.

- Reduce the cost of doing business and be extremely competitive by allowing small businesses to outsource back-office functions and only pay for the specific services they need. In other words, they do not have to hire back-office personnel when they can hire only the level of support they need when they need it.

- Become a recognized expert in business startup and growth. Consult to and mentor small-business owners.

- Build a strong network of experts in various types of specialties, so I could connect the companies I own and those I consult to with proven experts (be the person others call for just about any business topic — start, grow, or sell).

- Start a company that provides startup services to others where anyone who has an idea, wants to start a company, and wants to know how to go about it can come to our company for consultation and guidance.

- Help others expedite their company growth by providing them with tools, processes, procedures, templates, etc., so they do not have to reinvent the wheel.

- Provide training services.

- Write *how-to* books. (Read my book, *Start, Grow, Sell. A Primer for Starting, Growing and Selling Your Own Government Contracting Business.*)

- Network my company executives with others in my network, so they become better connected and can therefore grow faster by working together.

- Become a recognized expert in helping others to sell their companies.

- Learn all about the process of acquiring companies and become a go-to person (recognized acquisition expert) when others want to buy a company or sell their company.

- Buy companies using the profits of my companies.

- Give back personally of my time and resources.

- Foster an environment of giving back — of our profits, time, and resources (both technical and people).

These are actual bullet points I brainstormed in my early, private planning sessions. Over the years I have refined the original concepts a few times, just as I have refined my overall business concept every year to what it is today.

Extending My Vision through Strategic Partnerships

We started companies to do technical work, and we created companies to do the back-office services that take the burden off of the technical workers. In some cases, there already were companies in existence that perform the functions we were considering doing in our new starts. We created strategic partnerships with them rather than create a new company that would compete against them. This allowed us to create the same diversified dynamic without having to go through the sometimes-tedious process of starting up a new company and finding the right people to work for it.

My business concept may not have been entirely unique, but who ever said that your business idea has to be unique to be successful? I want to use my expertise and connections to continue to start new specialty companies with small-business certifications and offer services not only to my companies, but to other businesses as well.

My Future

The bulk of my early career focused on systems engineering and systems integration work, either in the Air Force or as an employee of a contractor company. I have spent the past several years starting and growing companies and diversifying my ownership into business, management and startup consulting, real estate investment (rehab, rentals), staffing and recruiting, contracts and finance services consulting, and marketing and branding.

Sounds like quite a leap, doesn't it? To go from serving in the Air Force to working as an employee for others to owning one company to being an owner in multiple companies! The thing that is most important to me is that I choose my own path; I set my own agenda; and I control my own schedule.

And I am not done! I have several companies in the queue that I plan to start over the next few years. I am confident, since I love what I do, I will start even more companies until I finally decide to retire, if that day ever comes.

My pastor gave me a compliment, when in a sermon in 2012 he said,

> *Tom Keith is one of the most driven, goal-oriented, get-it-done persons I have ever been around in my life!*

I do not know if I deserve all of that praise, but I am driven. I do set lofty goals, and I press on regardless of the roadblocks. I treat roadblocks as learning experiences.

> *I am not afraid of storms for I am learning how to sail my ship. — Louisa May Alcott*

I believe in having big visions. I have a vision for my businesses and my personal life. I know that I will run into hurdles, but I also know that I will continue to march toward my vision. I used the following quote earlier in this book, but it is worth repeating here:

> *If your vision doesn't scare you, then both your vision and your God are too small. — Brother Andrew*

I hope that you will be bold in your thinking, your vision, and your efforts, and I hope you will take action today, to get started toward your vision.

> *Whatever you can do, or dream you can do, begin it. Boldness has genius, power, and magic in it. Begin it now. — W.H. Murray*

Your Future

What does the future hold for you? Do you have special skills that you have mastered that you could turn into a business? As I said in the previous section, your business does not necessarily have to be unique, but you need to have some product or service that others want.

I know many people who have started businesses after mastering skills that others want. Here are examples of friends, acquaintances, and neighbors who have made the leap from employee to business owner by mastering their skills and starting their own business:

- A web developer went from creating and maintaining his company's and their clients' websites to starting his own LLC and running his own web services business.
- A blackbelt in taekwondo turned his love of this Korean martial art into his own school for teaching others.
- A neighbor who worked for a local parts store turned his love for working outdoors into his own lawn service.
- A stay-at-home mom turned her love for photography into a wedding photography business and she is now the primary breadwinner in the home.
- Another stay-home-mom turned her love of photography into a company that teaches others photography.
- A SharePoint developer started her own SharePoint services company, training others and providing SharePoint expertise to other companies in need.
- A contracts specialist started her own business to provide back-office support to small businesses.
- Fitness experts in my neighborhood created their own businesses providing personal trainer services.
- An expert pianist retired and started her own business providing piano lessons on her own schedule.
- A piano repairman started his own LLC providing in-home piano tuning and repair services.

But that's enough examples. The point is that I started my business model and my companies, and they started their own businesses too.

None of these business owners would have been able to be successful if they have not gotten their finances in order and built an emergency fund to fall back on and carry them through the early period when cash was tight. They worked hard to become experts in areas where others needed their skills. They learned enough about finances to make smart choices and they built teams of advisors, experts and mentors to help them get and stay successful.

All of these people can grow their own businesses as large as they choose to, and in some cases they have actually moved into franchising their businesses. Others are staying small by choice.

As business owners, that is their prerogative.

I understand that if you are living paycheck to paycheck, starting your own company sounds like an impossibility. But while you get your finances in order, spend your time learning and building your expertise at something you love to do. My work never seems like work because I love what I do.

I actually wake up early every day anxious to get started because this is what drives me. The last time I woke up completely dreading my work was when I was an employee. Now that I am in control and report to no one, I wake up every day excited to dig in.

So, what does *your future* hold for you? Will you become an expert and start your own company (or companies)?

Action Steps For You

1. If you have never started a company but want to understand the basic steps involved in starting a company, read Appendix A. Appendix A details some of the key decisions you need to make, explains how to register with all the proper authorities (federal, state, and/or local), and teaches you how to prepare the proper internal documentation to help further legitimize your business. If you go step by step, you will see that startup is not difficult to accomplish. The process can be time-consuming, but many steps can now be accomplished online.

   I have started several companies, and one of the things I do in my consulting business is mentor others as they start their own government contracting companies. I authored a book, *Start, Grow, Sell: A Primer for Starting, Growing and Selling Your Government Contracting Business*, and it is available on Amazon if you have an interest in government contracting. Many of the topics apply no matter what kind of company you will be starting, but that book is aimed primarily at those people interested in government contracting.

2. Reread the last section of this Step 7, *Your Future*, and think about what you love to do...what you are passionate about. I wake up every day anxious to dig into my *work* because it is something I truly love to do. Do you have something in your life that you are just as passionate about?

3. Do a web search on "are you ready to start your own business?" and you will find a lot of interesting articles and quizzes you can take to assess your readiness to start your own business.

4. Go to SBA.gov, the website for the U.S. Small Business Administration, and click on the link for *Starting and*

Managing and read through that section. The section outlines, from the big-picture perspective, what you need to do to start your own company and then manage that company. Read the articles and watch the videos. They even have training videos you can sign up for to help you understand and assess your readiness to start your own business.

5. Meet with those mentors and advisors I mentioned previously; talk to them about your ideas, and then outline your own high-level plan for your own business.

STEP 8: DIVERSIFY YOUR ASSETS

Diversification is key to my overall investment strategy. I have watched over the years as people put all of their money into one type of investment, such as their 401(k). They joined a company and set up their 401(k) and then they let their 401(k) just exist for years without rebalancing, realigning or diversifying. Then, when the market tanks, they take huge cuts. Only then do they take action. Usually that action is to panic and to sell everything and go to all cash thinking they won't lose more money. But selling their remaining stock and going to all cash only *assures* they lose money!

Or, they work their entire life under the assumption their employer will provide a nice pension they can retire on. I have a close relative who has worked for almost twenty-five years toward a retirement pension only to learn that the pension fund is in trouble and there are now new requirements being levied on the employees before they can retire and draw a pension. Instead of being able to draw some pension amount after working twenty-five years with the company, he has found out that the new rules added an age requirement. Now a person has to have both thirty years and be at least fifty-five years old to draw a pension.

To make it even worse, the pension plan is having such dire financial problems that his expected pension, when he can finally draw it, will be fifty percent less than he anticipated. This is hard news to swallow after spending nearly twenty-five years with that company. Unfortunately, he does not have a strongly diversified set of income streams to make up for this reduction in retirement benefit. So, he will have to work longer and save even more.

He has worked his entire life for this same company and he assumed he was working toward a specific retirement timeline and amount, only to find out the rules are changing and he has no control over any of it. That could happen to anyone.

Another person very close to me worked for over forty years for a company before retiring. He has a pension of a little over $800 a month. The good news is that he has very good medical benefits, but to have a pension of $800 a month to show for over forty years of work is a little mind-boggling to me. It just does not seem fair. He now lives on his $800 pension supported by social security. He did not diversify and he did not invest in other assets to support his retirement.

No one can afford to think their one pension or IRA or 401(k) will be enough to retire on without careful management and long-term care and feeding. I have never been one to believe in being single-threaded. I like backup plans and taking parallel paths to get me to my endgame. So diversifying and creating multiple streams of income comes naturally for me.

~~~~~~

With the stock market dropping the way it did ending the year 2015 and going into 2016, I am very happy to be diversified not only in my stock selections, but in my other investments and my companies as well. Sure, the rules may change for me too in some cases, but by diversifying I am limiting the impact of a single income stream being reduced or eliminated altogether. If one of my income streams were to be reduced by 50 percent, as in the case of my relative's pension, it will have a much lower impact on our overall income since we have diversified and created multiple streams to live on.

We've all read about the Enron Corporation debacle and how many people lost all of their money when Enron went under. That should not happen to anyone. But employees also have to take ownership of their own financial security and not have just one income stream they have no control over. I recognize that in the years past, people were more likely to spend their entire career in one company, but today people often work for multiple companies before they retire and they can take their retirement plans with them when they leave a company. They can then manage those plans to create multiple streams of income. Sadly, most people just let those retirement plans continue along without active management when they leave one company to join another.

I diversify within and across my various financial accounts — both retirement accounts and investment accounts. But I also diversify by investing in real estate and in company ownership. I started a few companies and I co-own a few other companies where I partnered with other experts in their fields. I also consult and advise through a separate legal entity, The Unconventional Strategist, that is wholly my own.

I can sleep at night knowing I keep my investments balanced. I'm not saying I never lose money; I do lose money sometimes *because* I invest. Investing involves risk, which means you make money sometimes and you lose money sometimes. But with investment brings reward when you actively stay on top of and diversify your investments.

Think of a diversified investment strategy as a barstool. Four or more legs pretty much keeps you very stable, but as you reduce the number of legs, the more you are at risk of falling down. I am diversified in that I own companies, real estate, investment portfolios, and retirement accounts. I also have a pension and eventually will be able to draw social security. But I do not want to rely on social security as I age.

Being diversified in such a way allows me (us) to sleep comfortably, because if one leg of our portfolio completely tanked, we would still be fine going into retirement. The chance that *every* element of our diversified investment strategy will tank is pretty low.

I diversified with *stocks and bonds ownership, individual company ownership,* and *real estate ownership.* My *barstool* has sufficient legs to balance us under almost any situation.

Stocks and Bonds Ownership

You can read online to learn about investing or go buy a book like one of these:

> *The Complete Idiot's Guide to Making Money on Wall Street* by Christy Heady

> *The Investing Bible* by Lynn O'Shaughnessy

> *Stock Market Investing for Beginners: Essentials to Start Investing Successfully* released by Tycho Press

> *The Intelligent Investor* by Benjamin Graham

> *Investing for Dummies* by Eric Tyson

There are so many options to learn the basics online or through reading books such as these, but the best way to get started investing is to just get started investing.

If you are new to investing in stocks and bonds, you may want to consider something like the Vanguard LifeStrategy Funds to get you started. You will have to decide how much risk you are willing to take for the potential reward of the investment. But, as you grow your investments and as you learn more about investing and your investing options, you can always partially or completely go to a stock and bond mix that you have researched and decided upon.

See this link for an overview of the family of funds:

https://investor.vanguard.com/mutual-funds/lifestrategy/#/

LifeStrategy Funds are tailored to the various kinds of investors based on risk level, whether new investors or long-time investors. For example:

> If you are a *low-to-moderate-risk investor* you can select the **LifeStrategy Income Fund**. This is typically for people who care most about income. With this fund you accept the limited growth that comes with the limited exposure to the stock market.

> If you are a *moderate-risk investor* you can select the **LifeStrategy Conservative Growth Fund**. This is typically for people who care more about current income then long-term growth. This is for people who want some growth potential but with less exposure to stock-market risk.

> If you are a *moderate-to-high-risk investor* you can select the **LifeStrategy Moderate Growth Fund**. This is typically for people who care most about growth than income. This is for people who want more growth potential and accept some added exposure to stock-market risk.

> If you are a *higher-risk investor* you can select the **LifeStrategy Growth Fund**. This is typically for people who care most about long-term. You accept the significant exposure to the stock market (and associated risks) in exchange for more growth potential.

I happen to like Vanguard and I use Vanguard, but most big investment houses today offer similar options to help get you started. Vanguard is set up to help the new investor or the long-term investor. I especially like that they favor the founder's philosophy — invest for the long term and stay in the market, keep the fees low, offer advice for those who need it, and be easy to use no matter your level of confidence in investing. You can grow with Vanguard and the services they offer are tailored to your needs. Of course, the more you have invested, the more incentive they offer you to use their experts to guide you in your investing.

With any of these options at Vanguard, you get broad diversification, automatic rebalancing, and low costs (one of the reasons I like Vanguard).

The key for you is to get started investing and invest regularly, whether you choose Vanguard or some other investment house.

Individual Company Ownership

I went over my company ownership strategy in detail in Step 3, so I won't repeat a lot here, but just as I diversify my sock investments, I also diversify my company ownership to allow for market fluctuations. So, as I write this, I own an engineering company, a back-office company (that specializes in areas like contracts and financial management), real estate (more on that in the next section), a few government-contracting companies with differing specialties of focus, and my consulting company. While I am a common denominator for the companies, they are all separate legal entities with separate profit/loss centers, each providing a diversified stream of income to me. That was and is my overall goal: to create multiple streams of income to achieve financial security. Even if one of my companies were to go under, I have the other companies to rely on. When one company struggles, usually the others make up for it.

My companies have grown to the point where they bring in millions of dollars of annual revenue, so if the real estate investments and my retirement accounts were to all fail, I still have the annual profits or eventual sale of my company ownership to provide financial security. Or, I can keep my ownership in the companies and live off of the profits until I die. Are you seeing how diversification works? If you have never started a company but want to understand the basic steps involved, read Appendix A.

Real Estate Ownership

My real estate strategy was to buy fixer-uppers so we could put sweat equity into the properties and give me something I could do and share with my family members. We bought properties close by that we could easily manage and maintain ourselves. We took a long-term view so as to let the renters pay the mortgage for us while building up more equity in the company. The original strategy we put together included taking profits from the properties and using that money to buy other properties, and then, over time, hiring someone else to manage the properties for us.

We protected our personal investments by owning the properties under the corporate structure of an LLC so that if we were ever sued for any reason, the individuals could be suing the LLC and not going after our personal assets. If you consider real estate as an approach to diversifying, you should consider a separate business entity such as an LLC for *each* company to protect the assets individually. This reduces risk for each asset as well as diversifies your streams of investments.

With interest rates so low these days, you can get shorter mortgages, and in fifteen to twenty years the properties are paid off, creating larger revenue streams or more opportunity to pull money and reinvest into other new properties or other diversified investment opportunities.

For years, real estate has protected us as investors from inflation and has been a great vehicle to grow and protect wealth. Real estate is also well-suited for generational wealth transfer under the current tax laws. Real estate is an asset that will always be in demand, so it may be a way for you to diversify your assets and investments as we did.

I won't say real estate investing is for everyone because dealing with renters can have its drawbacks, but it has paid off financially for us.

~~~~~~

You Should Diversify by Creating Additional Streams of Income Too

If you are dependent on one income, what will you do if that income ends? Or what will you do if, like my relative, you find out that your pension will only be 50% of what you anticipated? Are you prepared? Have you saved? Have you stayed out of debt? One thing I have learned is that most jobs are not guaranteed. Millions of people have been laid off over the last few years, but the good news is that if people are willing to work hard and put on their thinking caps, there are endless ways to create additional streams of income for their family. I work in a business world that I created. I started companies and I have worked hard to make sure they are successful so that we can live comfortably. I live according to my own business model that I created. You can too.

Many other people have started their own businesses, as part-time or full-time ventures. A neighbor of ours makes money by offering a dog-walking service for neighbors or friends, and she does that through an LLC. She is taking advantage of the corporate structure to save money and write off all legitimate business expenses. She has a SEP and funds her own retirement account.

Other neighbors are dentists, business consultants, personal yoga instructors, music instructors, etc. They wisely run their businesses through corporate structures and make the most of legitimate tax write-offs.

Take a look at what you have done. What you have learned. What you are good at and passionate about. What do you want to share with others? Are you like me and just want to live according to your own rules and work on your own schedule? The key is to think creatively and determine what skill or knowledge you have that others would pay for, and then focus on building it into a marketable concept and create a new income stream.

Diversify like I did. The more income streams you have, the easier it is to recover if one of them goes away or is reduced by 50 percent like my relative's future pension. Even now as I write this, I am creating another potential revenue stream for my family. This book may not sell enough to even cover my time, or it may sell very well. But in the end, I am writing this book primarily for my children to help to get them thinking about their future and their financial security. I want my children to realize that their financial security is their own responsibility and they should not count on the government to care for them during their retirement years. They too need to take ownership of their financial security and create diversified revenue streams to carry them through their retirement.

I am always looking for ways to create another revenue stream. I don't want to have to rely on just one revenue stream because I owe it to my wife to live up to my commitment to her to provide security for this family. If I only had a single revenue stream and it were to go away, we would be in trouble. If you have six or eight or even more revenue streams, then losing one revenue stream will be an irritant, but not life-altering.

Use Your Profits to Diversify Further by Funding Future Growth Streams

As you find yourself growing your resources, you have to decide what you will do with those growing resources. Will you buy more stock? I do buy more stock, but I believe in diversifying so I always look at ways to invest for growth in my existing companies or in other ventures that may create yet another potential stream of income. I may start another company from scratch. I've done that, so I already know how to start, grow, and sell a company. I authored a book of that very title, *Start, Grow, Sell: A Primer for Starting, Growing and Selling Your Government Contracting Business*, and it is available on Amazon.

I have partnered with and invested in other entrepreneurs who had specific technical skills and wanted to own their own company but did not know how to start, and then grow or manage, their own company. These entrepreneurs have the technical knowhow, but often do not know the business side of things and they do not have the financial resources to create a successful business. Part of my approach is to invest my time and resources in select companies and select people and then mentor them to success.

So you will have similar choices too. Do you just buy more stock? Do you reinvest profits back into your existing company (or companies)? Do you invest in other people? Other technology? How will you diversify to achieve financial security?

As you have money to invest and are considering your diversification options, be mindful of *opportunity cost* and the *rule of 72*, terms many financial advisors will be sure to tell you about. The rule of 72 is a very simple mathematical equation that teaches you how often your money will double over a period of time. The equation is simply this: 72 divided by the compound annual interest rate you earn equals the number of years required to double your investment. For example: if you earn 4 percent on your money, you would divide 72 by 4 and see that your money will double every 18 years. This equation is important for determining and projecting how your money could grow. The rule is also important for determining *opportunity cost*. To explain, consider the rule of 72 on the money you have sitting in the bank earning less than 1 percent interest. At 1 percent interest, it would take you 72 years for your money to double. If there is an opportunity for your money to grow at 6 percent, the opportunity cost is 5 percent (the difference between leaving your money in the account at 1 percent or investing and growing at 6 percent). Would you rather your money double every 72 years or every 12 years? The math helps you to see to see the opportunity you may be missing and consider that opportunity cost as you weigh the risk of the investment alternatives.

I believe in a well-balanced, diversified portfolio. I never want to be too heavily invested in any one investment, but I also do not want to be so conservative that my opportunity cost is very high and I essentially lose money.

Action Steps For You

1. Assess all of your holdings and investments; determine if you are diversified and well-balanced across your investments.

2. Consider this *partial list* of specific areas where I am invested as a way to diversify and protect my portfolio and see if some of these might work for you:

   o Dividend-paying stocks

   o Growth stocks

   o International stocks from healthy geographic regions

   o Speculative stocks

   o Gold

   o Bonds

   o Cash

   o Real estate (not just my primary residence)

   o Company ownership (I have ownership in more than one company that I started or co-started with partners. I have ownership in companies that I invested in.)

   o Intellectual property

   o Books (I have three more new books in the works as I write this.)

   o Photography (I am using my love of photography to create new streams of income in the form of books, plus individual photographs I will sell online.)

- o Pension (I have a government pension for my twenty years of service in the Air Force that, if I die, is set up to pass on to my wife.)

3. Think about my list and create your own plan of attack to continue to diversify and add new streams of income over your lifetime. Consider these ideas as you create your own diversification plan:

- o Songwriters and musicians earn royalties.

- o Authors earn royalties on every book they write.

- o Insurance agents can earn residual streams of income on the products they sell.

- o Actors can get paid a salary and a percentage of the sells.

- o Franchisors get franchise fee.

- o Software developers can get royalties for their products.

- o Inventors get royalties on the inventions.

- o Experts in their field get speaking fees that can be very profitable over time.

- o Business developers can get a percentage of the business they develop in our companies.

- o This list could go on for pages, but you get the idea.

STEP 9: PROTECT YOUR ASSETS

As I'm sure you do, I work very hard. I always have. I love what I do, I enjoy getting paid nicely for my work, and I want to be able to maximize my income and maximize my retained earnings. So I work just as hard to *keep* my money as I do to make it. I want to ensure my hard-earned money stays mine and can be passed on to my heirs and charities with the minimum tax impact possible. So I do everything I can to keep my money (e.g., reduce taxes) while I am alive and I want to make sure I can control (and maximize) how much I can pass on when I pass on.

I've talked about protecting my assets throughout this book, but I wanted to focus on it a little more specifically in this chapter. There are many things you can do to ensure your money stays your money (or your heirs'); some of these cost you money to implement and others just require a little effort on your part.

I'll cover several topics important to me and some that may apply to your situation as well. I'll start with the *importance of financial planning*, and then address how to use *business entities to protect your assets*, outline steps you should take to *protect your intellectual property*, and wrap up Step 9 by talking about *my personal written instructions to my heirs*.

FINANCIAL PLANNING: THE MOST IMPORTANT THING YOU CAN DO

I talked about financial planning in Step 4, but financial planning tops my list here because it doesn't matter how your wealth is made; without disciplined financial planning, your wealth could easily be lost to taxes, poor investments, high fees, etc.

If you leave a large lump sum to your dependents and they are not prepared in advance (and *you* have not prepared in advance), then your wealth could easily dissipate far more quickly than it took you to earn it.

If you haven't done so, stop right now and take stock of your investments and the protection plans you have in place.

I would recommend you also have an expert financial advisor review your situation. Get his or her advice for how better to diversify and protect your assets, now and in the future.

Do what I talked about throughout this book: take stock of your current situation, tally your assets, and then consider how far you are away from financial security. Put a focused plan in place to achieve financial security.

As I have learned the hard way, you have to take ownership of your own financial security. Financial security does not happen by accident. It takes a lot of work and a lot of your focused attention.

I'm repeating myself on purpose, but the earlier you get started, the better; if you put a long-term plan in place and stay focused on your goals, you can achieve financial security.

For me, it was important that I learned enough about financial planning, finances, and investing to make sure I understood my options. I did not want to rely on others. My wife would say that is a control problem of mine, but whatever you want to call it, I firmly believe that my financial security is wholly in my hands. I can't control the market swings, but I can learn enough to make my own educated decisions and not be at the mercy of a financial advisor.

If you decide to use a financial advisor then you need to understand enough about finances and investing to be able to consider the options the advisor presents to you and then make an informed decision.

So start now to invest in your financial education and make sure your heirs also invest in their financial education so they don't mismanage the wealth they eventually inherit.

I learned a lot of what I know about investing and asset protection over the last twenty years by reading and by investing. I hope my family members have learned some things from me over the years, but I have learned so much more now that the children are all grown and out of the house, which is another reason I wanted to write this book. They are no longer here in the house where I can try to impart my education, so I need to encourage from afar and hopefully pass on some of my learning though my writing.

Part of Financial Planning Is to Consider the Insurance You Own and the Insurance You Need to Own

I talked about this previously, but you can be insurance-poor (just as some people are mortgage-poor: meaning they spend so much on their mortgage they don't have any money to do anything else) if you are not careful. So learn enough about what insurance you need and make sure you have the right insurance in place and the proper amount of coverage. Don't even get me started on how much unnecessary insurance my dad was sold (and maintained) over the years by his so-called friend and insurance agent. But I digress. Insurance — the right insurance and the right amount of insurance — is very important in protecting you and your assets.

Talk to your financial advisor and your accountant and get their assessment of what insurance you *should* own.

Do not just talk to your insurance agent to get their opinion of what insurance you need, because they make money by selling you insurance products. So you want to get independent assessments of the insurance you own and the insurance you need to own.

Don't misunderstand me: you *do* need insurance. It's just that we live in a litigious society and you need to have the right insurance to protect you and your assets. You also don't want to over-insure and waste the money you could be saving and investing.

Here are several types of insurance you should know about:

Homeowners Insurance protects you if someone gets hurt on your property; it protects you in the event of home theft, and so much more. Talk to your insurance agent to get a complete list of homeowner insurance benefits. Choose a deductible you can pay out of your savings, and make sure liability coverage is adequate in case someone gets hurt on your property and decides to sue you.

Liability Insurance. As your net worth grows, make sure you increase your liability insurance to be adequately covered.

Auto Insurance. Buy enough auto insurance coverage so that you will have meaningful protection in the event your vehicle is involved in an accident and generates a lawsuit. You should make sure your total liability coverage is at least equal to your total assets.

Umbrella Coverage. Umbrella coverage is additional backup insurance that can be used in the instance that your other policies are inadequate. In the event that your auto, homeowners, or other liability policies are exhausted, umbrella coverage pays benefits up to the limit of the policy you bought. So you need to annually review your insurance needs and make sure you are adequately protected.

Long-Term Care Insurance. We have long-term care insurance to protect us against the financially devastating costs of in-home or nursing home care for chronic ailments, such as Alzheimer's, strokes, and the like. My mother and her father both had Alzheimer's and we are well aware of the high cost of such care.

Life Insurance. Term life is so cheap these days, there is almost no reason not to have ample term insurance in place in case something unfortunate happens. If you are a single-income family like we were (are) and lose the income earner, have you set aside sufficient resources to care for you family? Over the years we carried a minimum of a $1,000,000 policy to protect my wife and children while they were relying on my income. If something had happened to me during the period where we had not saved sufficient resources, my family would have struggled to get by.

~~~~~

USE BUSINESS ENTITIES TO PROTECT YOUR ASSETS

If you are an entrepreneur like I am, it's important to separate your personal assets from those in your business. You should take the specific legal steps to create a separate business entity, such as a corporation, limited liability company (LLC), or limited partnership, because even the simplest business dispute could well cost you everything you own.

You should carefully choose a legal entity *type* for your business, but each entity type has two important implications regarding how to deal with taxes and protection from creditors and lawsuits. So, first, let's look at those two implications in general, and as we do, we'll look at specific entity types and talk more about taxes and protection.

1. Tax advantages

As an employee, first you pay the government (i.e., get taxed), and then you live on what is left. Tax is a major expense and should be minimized as far as legally possible.

Earnings are taxed last, which means the government only receives their share of your income last. You benefit by living on pre-tax dollars.

Individuals: Earn - Pay taxes - Live on the remainder

Companies: Earn - Deduct expenses – Pay taxes on the remainder

Conducting business in a company at a lower tax rate minimizes your tax expense, which means you have more resources to spend on income-generating assets.

2. Protection

A second advantage offered by a corporation is protection from creditors and lawsuits.

Doing business in your personal name, you own and control everything. Someone can simply sue you to get their hands on it, provided their allegations can be proved in a court of law.

In a company, you own nothing, but control everything. Depending on how you structure your company, corporations can be used to add multiple layers of protection around your assets.

So, corporations are not only there for the wealthy, but rather for anybody who wants to own and protect their income-generating assets.

Here's a look at the different business types and their impact on taxes:

A. Sole Proprietorship. A single person owns and maintains complete control of the business.

> **Liability.** The owner of the business is solely liable for the actions and debts of the business. The owner's assets are at risk when legal action is brought against the business, which is one of the biggest downsides of a sole proprietorship.

Taxes. Income and expenses are reported on the personal tax return of the owner.

This model can be attractive because potential losses of the business can be used to offset income from other sources and reduce the owner's overall tax burden. Another upside is that the income from the business is taxed only once, as opposed to income from other entities that will be taxed twice (see Section D, Corporation). In addition to paying taxes on income, a sole proprietor must pay self-employment taxes, which are calculated using Schedule SE when filing a personal tax return.

B. General Partnership. Very similar to a sole proprietorship, a **general partnership** is also referred to simply as a **partnership** and is often used when two or more individuals own and control a business. In a general partnership, all partners take an active role in running the business.

Liability. As with a sole proprietorship, each owner in a partnership is individually responsible for all debts of the business. Responsibility is not in proportion to ownership, which means one partner may be responsible for the entire debt if no other partners have the assets to help repay a debt. For this reason, partnerships can be viewed as too high-risk and are not generally a preferred entity choice.

Taxes. As with a sole proprietorship, a partnership is not taxed as a separate entity and the income or losses from the business *pass through* to the individual partners. The income or losses are filed using Form 1065, and each partner uses Schedule K-1 to report their share of the business income. One upside of a partnership is that, at the end of the year, partners are allowed to divide up the profits and losses as they see fit. This means that if the partnership operates at a loss, and one partner has an otherwise relatively high income, then most or all of the partnership's loss may be allocated to that partner to reduce their tax burden.

This flexibility may be very appealing for owners with various situations as long as they balance the liability implications.

C. Limited Partnership. This is a specific type of partnership in which one or more of the partners are passive investors who do not take part in the day-to-day operation of the business. These investors are known as **limited partners**, while the controlling partners are known as **general partners**.

Liability. General partners maintain personal liability for all debts of the business, while the liability of limited partners is limited to the amount of their investment in the business.

Taxes. Taxes are handled very similarly to a general partnership, except that the amount of losses a limited partner may claim are limited. In reality, limited partnerships can be complicated and expensive to establish. For this reason they can be impractical, and businesses rarely opt for this legal designation.

D. Corporation. A regular corporation, or C Corporation **(C-Corp),** is one of the more complicated and expensive ways to run a business, but it does offer advantages. Once created (incorporated), a corporation becomes a separate entity from its owners that continues in perpetuity in the eyes of the law. Owners of the corporation, also known as shareholders, elect a board of directors that will effectively manage the day-to-day operations of the company. One of the main advantages of the corporate structure is the ability to raise funds by issuing new stock to sell to potential shareholders.

Liability. Since a corporation is a separate entity in the eyes of the law, the shareholders in the company are not generally liable for the company's debts and obligations outside of the amount they invest in the company.

This protection is part of what makes the corporation model appealing.

Taxes. As a corporation is treated as its own legal entity, it is treated as such for tax purposes. This means that all income is taxed on the corporate level, and then shareholders pay income tax again when they receive dividends. This *double taxation* is one of the biggest downsides of the corporate structure. One way to lessen the amount of tax paid is to pay a reasonable salary to shareholders who take an active role in the company, therefore reducing the amount of total profit that the corporation actually makes. Also, the corporation has the choice to retain earnings for re-investment as opposed to distributing all earnings to the shareholders, which is another way to mitigate personal income taxes, even if it is a short-term solution.

Professional Corporation (PC). This is a special type of corporation that may be used in professions requiring a license to practice, such as attorneys, physicians, architects, etc. This type of corporation does not provide liability protection for its owner(s) against professional negligence/malpractice.

> **Seek legal advice before choosing an entity type!**
>
> If your profession requires a license to practice, it is *strongly* recommended that you consult with a lawyer before choosing an entity type for your business.

E. Subchapter S Corporation. Also known as an S Corporation or **S-Corp**, a Subchapter S Corporation is very similar to a C-Corp, but it offers some very distinct advantages as well as some limitations. First, shareholders of S-Corps must be individuals, estates, or certain kinds of trusts. This means that an S-Corp cannot be owned by another entity such as a C-Corp, LLC, etc. The one exception to this rule is that one S-Corp may own another qualified S-Corp as a Qualified Subchapter S Subsidiary **(QSSS)** as long as it owns 100 percent of the shares of the subsidiary as defined under Title 26, Section 1361 of the U.S. Code. Additionally, S-Corps are limited to no more than 100 shareholders, making them better suited for small businesses. One downside is that S-Corps may only issue one class of stock, whereas C-Corps are able to customize and issue various different classes of stock, such as preferred or common stock.

Liability. As with a C-Corp, shareholders' liability is generally limited to the amount they have invested in the company.

Taxes. S-Corps offer many tax advantages over C-Corps, which makes them a popular choice for small-business owners. First and foremost, income from an S-Corp passes through to the individual shareholders' tax returns, therefore eliminating the double-taxation that occurs with the standard corporation. S-Corps can also take advantage of the **cash** method of accounting, whereas C-Corps must use the **accrual** method.

Cash Accounting. In cash accounting, money is recorded on the books at the time it is actually paid out or received. For example, if you sell a product in December 2013 but do not receive payment for said product until January 2014, the sale goes on the books in January and the income is counted for the 2014 year (assuming you use the calendar year as your fiscal year).

Accrual Accounting. In accrual accounting, money is recorded when it is actually *earned*. In the above example, since the product was sold in December, that is when the income is recorded for tax purposes even though payment has not actually been received.

F. Limited Liability Corporation (LLC). The LLC is a relatively new, yet highly popular, entity choice for new businesses that combines some of the best aspects of partnerships and corporations. In most ways, an LLC is very similar to an S-Corp except that there is no limitation on the number of owners or members in an LLC.

Liability. Much like a corporation, an LLC is its own separate entity, which means that members' liability is limited to the amount of their investment.

Taxes. Flexibility is a key benefit of an LLC. LLC owners can choose whether they wish to be taxed as a corporation or as a partnership. More and more, new LLC owners file to be taxed as an S-Corp.

Consider the tax implications of your entity type!

I strongly recommend that you talk to your tax advisor and accountant about the tax implications for your specific situation.

Limited Liability Partnership (LLP). Similar to a professional corporation, this entity type is often used for professions that require a license to practice. The key difference between an LLP and an LLC is that the partners in an LLP may be held personally liable for their own negligence. An LLP does, however, protect partners from being held liable for the negligence of other partners in the company.

~~~~~

PROTECT YOUR INTELLECTUAL PROPERTY

[This section is a summary of some of the more detailed material you can find in my book, *Start Grow Sell, A Primer for Starting, Growing and Selling Your Government Contracting Business*. Start Grow Sell is available on Amazon.]

I've already shown that in business, protecting your assets is essential. It's why companies opt to do business as a Limited Liability Company **(LLC)** or Corporation and why they purchase insurance to cover everything from company vehicles to the very lives of the owners. As a business owner, you have many assets besides the physical ones that may come to mind, such as money, real estate, or machinery. You also have the right to protect your intellectual property **(IP)** — intangible assets that your business owns and controls — from your name and logo to a secret recipe or even a unique business process. Protecting your IP is such an important topic that I wanted to discuss the various types of IP and the means of protection available in some detail.

The different forms of IP tend to overlap, but they are typically grouped into two main categories: **functional** and **non-functional**. Functional IP includes **utility patents** and **trade secrets**; non-functional IP includes **trademarks and service marks, design patents, copyrights,** and **trade dress.** The best way to think about it is that functional IP rights protect those aspects of a product or idea that actually make it *work*. On the other hand, non-functional IP rights protect those aspects that are purely aesthetic and do not improve actual function in any way.

For example: imagine you develop a new refrigerator. If you invent a new technology that improves the temperature regulation and reduces energy expenditure, then you could protect this highly *functional* aspect through a utility patent. On the other hand, the aesthetic aspects such as the sleek handle design or even the name would be protected through the *non-functional* IP protections of design patents and trademarks, respectively.

Now that you have a basic understanding of what separates the two sides of IP, let's break it down further as I introduce each of the individual aspects of IP rights.

1. FUNCTIONAL

As a reminder, functional IP is designed to protect the *functional* aspects of a product and includes utility patents and trade secrets.

A. Utility Patents

According the U.S. Patent and Trademark Office **(PTO)**, utility patents are "issued for the invention of a new and useful process, machine, manufacture, or composition of matter, or a new and useful improvement thereof . . . ." (http://www.uspto.gov/web/offices/ac/ido/oeip/taf/patd esc.htm) This grants the patent owner the *exclusive right to make, use, and sell the invention for up to twenty years*. It also gives the owner the legal right to seek damages from anybody who violates the patent by making, using, or selling the invention.

The types of inventions that qualify for a patent are as follows:

- **Process.** A unique and definable series of steps that can be followed to achieve a certain result.

- **Machine.** A piece of equipment that achieves results through the interaction of its different parts.

- **Manufacture,** also referred to as an **Article of Manufacture.** This can refer to one of two different types of objects. The first is a single object that simply does not have any moving parts like a paperweight or bookend. The second is an object that has moving parts that are not essential to the usefulness of the object. An example of this would be a folding knife, where the ability of the knife to cut (its intended use) is independent of its ability to open and close.

- **Composition of Matter.** A specific combination of chemicals or materials, such as household cleaners or lubricants.

- **Improvements.** A specific improvement on a previous invention of one of the previous listed types.

In order to receive a patent, an invention must meet three criteria. It must be:

- **Useful,** and the purpose of the invention must not be illegal or deceptive.

- **Novel,** as in it must truly be an invention and not something that is already known about or used by other people.

- **Non-obvious,** perhaps the most subjective and hardest criterion to define. Generally speaking, it must be something that others in the field would not necessarily expect or maybe even think could be achieved.

Patents generally are considered one of the most powerful aspects of IP because of the potential licensing power. I will cover licensing more in depth later, but it is important to note that it is a primary method of capitalizing on your ideas. The process of obtaining a patent is known as **prosecution**. You must file a written application that thoroughly describes the invention so that someone who is educated in the field may reasonably duplicate it. While under review at the PTO, the invention can be referred to as "patent pending." Once granted, the patent is considered prosecuted.

Obtaining and maintaining a patent can be expensive — to the tune of tens of thousands of dollars. Costs can escalate because prosecution often calls for the services of patent lawyers, and once gained, patents require yearly fees to maintain. You should weigh all the costs and benefits of a patent before beginning the prosecution process.

B. Trade Secrets

Trade secrets are governed in the United States by the Uniform Trade Secrets Act **(UTSA)**. According to the UTSA, "**Trade secret** means information, including a formula, pattern, compilation, program, device, method, technique, or process, that:

a. Derives independent economic value, actual or potential, from not being generally known to, and not being readily ascertainable by proper means by, other persons who can obtain economic value from its disclosure or use, and

b. Is the subject of efforts that are reasonable under the circumstances to maintain its secrecy."

In other words, a trade secret is information used by your business to gain an economic advantage over the competition. Unlike a patent, where you are required to publicly disclose the invention and how it works, trade secrets demand that you make all reasonable efforts to keep the important information private and undisclosed. Once you have willfully disseminated the information to the public, that information loses its status as a trade secret.

As you are expected to preserve your trade secret, there is no application process similar to that of obtaining a patent. Instead, you are expected to protect the trade secret through physical, technological, and legal means (such as using non-disclosure agreements **[NDA]**). Your protection comes through the ability to seek legal action against those who acquire your trade secret through improper means. According to the UTSA, "**Improper means** includes theft, bribery, misrepresentation, breach or inducement of a breach of a duty to maintain secrecy, or espionage through electronic or other means."

This standard puts the burden of proof on the original holder of the trade secret to show that they had taken reasonable measures to ensure the protection of their trade secret, and also that it was actually stolen through improper means. Unlike with a patent, the UTSA provides no protection for trade secrets when these criteria are not met. This approach means that if somebody else legitimately reverse-engineers or independently invents your trade secret, then you lose all protection.

2. NON-FUNCTIONAL

As a reminder, non-functional IP protects those aspects of a product that are purely aesthetic and includes trademarks and service marks, design patents, copyright, and trade dress.

A. Trademarks and Service Marks

As with patents, trademarks are controlled by the U.S. Patent and Trademark Office. According to the PTO, "A **trademark** is a word, phrase, symbol, and/or design that identifies and distinguishes the source of the goods of one party from those of others. A **service mark** is a word, phrase, symbol, and/or design that identifies and distinguishes the source of a service rather than goods. The term 'trademark' is often used to refer

to both trademarks and service marks."
(www.uspto.gov/trademarks/basics/definitions.jsp)

There are several important things to know about trademarks that set them apart from other forms of IP. First, trademarks are not related to the creation of a product or idea so much as they are related to one's ability to sell their goods and services. As the main goal of a trademark is to identify the source of a product being sold, you must actually sell or advertise your product in order to obtain legal protection. The only way to obtain trademark protection without selling or advertising a product is to file an **Intent-to-Use Registration**, in which case, you must be able to show that you intend to use the trademark in federally regulated commerce in the near future.

Second, trademarks do not have to be registered to gain legal protection. Trademarks are regulated at the federal level as opposed to the state level. This means that you must use your trademark in federally regulated commerce — for instance, internationally or even just across state lines — in order to register with the PTO. Even then, the question of whether or not to register your trademark is up to you. If you only sell your goods or services within a single state or if you simply choose not to register, then your mark will still be protected under common law.

The benefits of registering include use of the registered trademark symbol ®, as well as creating the assumption that you have the right to use that mark nationally. The downside to registering is that you have to pay fees and renew the registration periodically. If your trademark is unregistered, then you must use the symbol ™ for trademark or ˢᴹ for service mark.

Third, trademarks are primarily controlled by the right of first use as opposed to being controlled by registration. To put it simply, you gain legal protection of a trademark the very first day that you use it in commerce. This means that if somebody else comes along and registers a mark that is the same as or very similar to yours after you have been using it, you will retain the right to use the mark even though they registered and you did not. You simply have to be able to show that you were using the mark first, in which case you can petition to cancel the other company's registration or even take them to court to pursue legal action.

Finally, it is important to note that there is no time limit for trademark protection. As long as you use the trademark in commerce, you will continue to enjoy the legal protections and the exclusive right to use that trademark.

B. Design Patents

Design patents are very similar to utility patents, and are also controlled by the PTO. The primary difference is that design patents exist to protect the purely aesthetic, or ornamental, aspects of an otherwise functional or utilitarian design. To acquire a design patent, the design must be new, original, and ornamental. For example, if you designed a children's television that looked like a monkey, you could obtain a design patent for the monkey design as it is purely ornamental and does not affect the functionality of the television itself. Design patents last fourteen years and must be filed within a year of the date that you first begin selling the product.

C. Copyright

In the United States, the Copyright Act of 1976 primarily governs copyright law. Generally speaking, the purpose of the copyright law is to protect and encourage the creation of artwork. It does so by granting the author of original art the exclusive right to reproduce and sell the artwork. As listed in the Copyright Act, the following categories of art and expression are eligible for copyright protection:

- Literary works
- Musical works, including any accompanying words
- Dramatic works, including any accompanying music
- Pantomimes and choreographic works
- Pictorial, graphic, and sculptural works
- Motion pictures and other audiovisual works
- Sound recordings
- Architectural works

(www.copyright.gov/title17/92chap1.html#102)

It is important to note that, as with design patents, there are aspects of products that you may want to garner copyright protection for, such as packaging or artwork included on the invention itself or in advertising. Copyright protection generally lasts quite a long time. For individual creators, a copyright will last for the duration of their lives plus seventy years. For copyrighted material created by a company, protection lasts for ninety-five years after first publication or 120 years after creation, whichever is longer.

D. Trade Dress

Trade dress, very similar to trademark and copyright law, prevents people from packaging products in ways that mimic the goods of another product. The protection strives to benefit the original maker of a product and also to safeguard customers from purchasing one item when they believe it is actually another item.

As with trademarks, you do not have to register with the PTO to gain protection, but you may do so if you choose. In order to gain protection, the design must be distinctive — that is, easily identifiable. It must also convey a "secondary meaning" in that the design creates an association with the producer in the mind of the consumer.

3. LICENSING AND ASSIGNMENTS

Now that you have a good idea of the various forms of IP, let's explore different ways of monetizing your ideas. If you have invented a product or created a piece of art, the most obvious and simple way to make money would be to obtain a patent or copyright and sell the products yourself. For various reasons, this is not always the easiest thing to do. Perhaps you do not have the time or resources to efficiently produce, market and sell the product yourself. Fortunately, odds are, there is someone out there who does have the resources necessary to accomplish this.

A. Licensing

Licensing makes this exchange possible. Simply put, a **license** is a contract in which you grant someone else the permission to use or produce and sell your invention for a specific period of time. In exchange for the rights to your invention, the **licensee** pays you, the **licensor**, fees known as royalties. As with any contract, licensing agreements can be written or oral, although written contracts are always recommended so as to avoid confusion later.

Licensing agreements can take on many forms and run the gamut from very simple to very complicated. Entire books are devoted to ways to write and implement licensing agreements. The contract can last for a certain amount of time or into perpetuity (or at least for as long as you retain protection under IP laws). An agreement can even be limited to certain geographic areas. For example, you can have a licensing agreement with one person to sell your product in

California and an agreement with somebody else to sell it in Texas.

There are also many ways to arrange for payment of royalties, and every method comes with inherent risks and benefits for each side. For instance, a single **lump-sum** payment at the beginning could be risky for both sides. If the sum is too small and the product takes off, then the licensor could lose a lot of potential profit. If the sum is too high and the product is not successfully marketed, then the licensee could end up with no return on a large investment.

With **per-unit** payment, the licensee pays a set amount of money per unit sold. This is also risky because either side could lose out depending on market fluctuations. For example, if the per-unit royalty is $5 and the profit margin only turns out to be $4, then the licensee not only loses money on each transaction but also loses incentive to sell the product. This scenario would be especially unfortunate because nobody would be making money even though the potential for profit exists.

The most popular licensing agreement allows for payments based on **net sales**. For each unit sold, the licensor receives a royalty payment as a percentage of the profit from that sale. This method tends to be the best balance of risk and reward for both sides, as neither is taking too large of a risk and both sides have the potential to make a lot of money if the product sells well. There are more payment models, and if you find yourself in the position of licensee or licensor, you should research the options and weigh the risks and rewards carefully.

B. Assignment

One last option to keep in mind is **assignment.** When you assign your rights to an invention, you permanently transfer those rights to another person. If we equate licensing to renting your house to a tenant for a specific period of time in exchange for rent money, then assignment is the equivalent of permanently selling your house and transferring your ownership rights to another person. This practice is not as common as licensing, though you may sometimes see the two terms used interchangeably. In legal terms, licensing and assignment are actually different, so when you hear the two terms, be sure to know which one is truly meant.

In the world of business, it is very important that you protect your assets. Oftentimes your intangible assets are far more valuable than your tangible ones, and your intangible assets are the real basis for your potential to earn a profit. Hopefully by reading this you will start to get an idea of where you might be vulnerable and what steps you need to take to protect your product, your intellectual property, and your business.

~~~~~

SPECIFIC PROTECTIONS COMPANIES CAN OFFER

There are many additional benefits and asset protection options to consider as *business owners, key personnel, and executives* that can be critical to your continued success. Here are a few benefits you may want to consider offering or putting in place. The company can pay for these benefits, but like all benefits, the costs affect the bottom-line rate you charge customers and your profit margins.

> **Buy-Sell Agreements.** If you start your company with one or more partners, I strongly recommend you set up and sign a buy-sell agreement *up front* – that is, as you start your company. You must know the terms inside and out! A buy-sell agreement defines how an owner's interest is to be distributed if he or she dies or becomes permanently disabled. This agreement helps ensure that a business or

professional practice can continue after the death or disability of one of the owners or partners. It does this by requiring each owner or partner to sell his or her interest to the remaining owners, or to the business entity itself, under terms defined in the agreement. The agreement equally obligates the remaining owners or the business entity to purchase the deceased or disabled owner's interest, and it stipulates the formula by which the price will be determined. The formula is negotiated and agreed upon in advance of the event, and the owners sign the document.

Key-Person Insurance. The main purpose of key-person insurance is to provide a death benefit to the business in the event of the premature death of an essential employee, but it can also be used as a way to provide the key person with supplemental non-qualified retirement benefits. With key-person insurance, a business purchases life insurance on the life of an essential employee to help the company survive financially if something happens to that individual.

Disability Buy-Out Plans. Disability buy-out insurance, which ensures a disabled business owner receives fair market value for his/her interest in the business, should be part of any business continuation or succession plan. A disability buy-out insurance plan provides the funds needed to purchase an owner's or partner's interest in the business if they become disabled. At the same time, the insurance protects all the business owners from the threat a disability could impose on the company by allowing them to buy out the disabled owner's interest — at an agreed-upon price set forth in a well-designed buy-sell agreement.

Deferred Executive Compensation. Non-qualified deferred compensation arrangements allow employers to reward selected executives without taking on the administrative burdens of qualified plans. In many cases, deferred compensation is used in addition to qualified retirement plans, and other broadly based employee benefit plans.

Executive Long-Term Care. An executive long-term care plan can be used when a business decides to reward a specific group of executives by purchasing a long-term care insurance policy for each member in the group. These executives usually are considered essential to the success of the business.

Executive Bonus Agreement. Employers usually find retaining and rewarding existing key employees more cost-effective than recruiting and training new employees. A properly structured executive bonus agreement can be an excellent tool for recruiting, retaining, and rewarding key employees.

Commercial Liability Insurance protects your business if someone gets hurt on the business premises, or is injured as the result of an action by another employee.

Worker's Compensation Insurance is mandatory in most jurisdictions. Worker's compensation protects you and your workers alike by ensuring that there's enough liquidity in place to take care of any employee who gets hurt on the job, and that the expenses don't come out of your pocket.

~~~~~

MY PERSONAL SET OF INSTRUCTIONS TO MY HEIRS – I CALL IT THE "BLUE SEDAN LETTER"

I take financial planning and protecting my assets very personally, and I have taken some very specific personal and business steps to outline my financial plans and protect my assets. I have written and maintain very clear instructions to my wife and beneficiaries should I pass away or become incapacitated. You too should have written instructions that guide your heirs through your wishes and desires should something happen to you. This is more than your legal will; this document is more personal and more specific about your finances, your business, and the protection you have put in place should something happen to you. I started this letter while I was on active duty in the Air Force and I update this letter every year or so as key elements of our financial situation change. I call this letter my *Blue Sedan Letter*.

Why do I call it a *Blue Sedan Letter*? In my Air Force days we were encouraged to write a personal letter to our spouse and heirs, in advance, should something happen to us. The letter was essentially step-by-step instructions written by the service member to the spouse or family member with step-by-step instructions the spouse or family member should follow if they received such news that the service member was killed in action (KIA) or missing in action (MIA). In times like those, the Air Force would send someone to the home of the deceased or MIA in a blue Air Force sedan to give the family the sad news. It was after the Air Force members arrived in the blue sedan that the surviving family members would read the letter their loved one had prepared for them. People typically dreaded seeing an Air Force blue sedan arrive at their home because if the service member was off in a war zone, it usually meant bad news was being delivered.

If you write such a letter, and I encourage you to do so, it is important that your heirs know where this letter is because should something happen to you, they are going to be in such an emotional state that they may not be able or ready to deal with all of the financial questions that will confront them.

My wife and heirs know exactly where to find my Blue Sedan Letter and it is in it that I tell them my most important wishes (things that don't necessarily need to be in the will). For instance, my Blue Sedan Letter tells everyone:

- Where my will is located and who all has a copy

- Where I want my ashes scattered

- How to reach my insurance agents for the various insurance policies in place

- Who my business partners are and how to reach each of them

- Who specifically needs to be notified as soon as possible and who can be notified in time

- The location of all of the critical paperwork tied to our personal lives

- The location of all of the critical paperwork tied to my work

It is not only important to *write* the Blue Sedan Letter, it is important that you *update* it regularly.

You can make the Blue Sedan Letter as complicated or as simple as possible. One of the main reasons to write the letter is because if something were to happen to you, your spouse will be distraught and confused and this simple letter will make it so much easier for your spouse to know exactly what to do and in what order. You don't want your spouse to be struggling with understanding the financial situation on top of losing you. My wife and I talk about these things and she knows exactly where to find the letter I wrote to her. You may want it to be a joint letter you compose together; the choice is yours.

Every year you should update your Blue Sedan Letter and reevaluate your financial plan, and with the help of advisors, make the necessary adjustments to ensure your wealth is protected. Your plan should outline what you have in place, what you are working on putting in place over the next few years. Your plan should also outline how the wealth is protected and how the wealth should be managed (and invested for future generations). The plan should incorporate tax-planning strategies to minimize the effect taxes will have on the wealth over generations.

As your wealth grows, make sure your financial advisor (or advisors) has the experience and expertise in working with your new level of assets. You should seek a financial planning expert who specializes in your area of focus as well as one who has experience working with your level of wealth. Consider an estate planning attorney and tax advisor who have a lot of experience with these amounts and with the appropriate strategies to help you manage your assets. There are advisors who are experts in helping you with smaller sums of money, and then there are experts that have experience advising their clients with $5 million, $10 million or more. The point is to make sure your advisors have the knowledge and experience to help *you*.

Action Steps For You

1. The first thing you need to do is assess your current asset-protection components, determine the protection you need, and then get the protection in place.

2. Ask yourself: are you protected at home and at work? If you own a business, you should have separate insurance in place to further protect your assets.

3. Review the insurance you have in place today. Is it still needed? Is it still adequate for your current situation? Reassess your insurance needs at least annually.

4. Talk to your insurance agent(s) regularly to make sure you are protected. Remember they make money by selling you insurance; your job is to understand what insurance you need and get the right amount of insurance in place. But before you buy or change your insurance …

5. Talk to a financial advisor to get their perspective too. Get that second or third opinion before changing your protection or before you buy any other insurance.

6. Ask yourself: do you have intellectual property and is it adequately protected?

7. Ask yourself: do you have all of your legal documents in place (such as a will, powers of attorney, etc.), and does someone know where those critical files are?

8. Have you written your own Blue Sedan Letter and let people close to you know where that letter is? If you pass away, they will be in distress and this will ease the burden of helping them figure out what to do and whom to call, because you have thoroughly documented it and maintained it in a safe place where they can get to it immediately.

STEP 10: USE EVERY LEGAL TAX ADVANTAGE YOU CAN TO KEEP YOUR MONEY

I own businesses for several reasons; one of the reasons, besides wanting to create diversified income streams, is to help me maximize my earning potential while minimizing my taxes. I believe in operating within the law, but like any good businessman, I am not shy about taking every legal tax advantage I can to cut my taxes and retain my hard-earned money. People who know me can attest to the fact that I work very hard for my money. I always have. But now I work for me, and for my family's financial security. Now that I look at money much differently than I did years ago, there is *even more reason* to fight to keep that hard-earned money.

You can read the Internal Revenue Service (IRS) Internal Revenue Code (IRC) yourself, but put simply, the IRC says that just about any expenditure used to produce business income is deductible. The IRS says that to be a deductible business expense, the expense must be:

- Ordinary and necessary for the business,

- Not extravagant, and

- Primarily for the business.

Essentially that means, *any money you spend in a reasonable way, with an expectation of bringing revenue into your business, is a deductible expense.*

I encourage you to go to the library and read (or better yet, buy for yourself), *Tax Savvy for Small Business* by tax attorney

Frederick Daily. While this is written for the small-business owner, it clearly outlines year-round tax strategies to save you money and it does so in plain language that anyone can understand.

Daily explains the top deduction categories for business owners, and how properly and legally utilizing just the deductions for these categories can save you a lot of money:

- Vehicles

- Equipment

- Inventory

- Home Offices

- Retirement Savings

- Costs of Going into Business

- Costs of Not Going into Business

- Accounting, Legal, and Other Professional Fees

- Supplies

- Entertainment and Meals

- Gifts

- Travel

- Moving Expenses

- Health Insurance

- Disability and Sick Pay

- Education Expenses

- Interest

- Bad Debts

- Charitable Contributions

- Taxes

- Advertising and Promotion

- Repairs and Improvements

- Business Insurance

- Research Expenditures

- General Business Credit

I believe in using the tax code to minimize my taxes. It helps that I have a great accountant to make sure I follow the letter of the law, but it also helps that I have spent a good amount of time reading and trying to understand how to use the tax laws to minimize my taxes. You too should make this a priority if you hope to keep more of your hard-earned money.

Remember what I said before: as an employee, first you pay the government (i.e., get taxed), and then you live on what is left (post-tax dollars). As an employee, the more promotions you get or the harder you work, the more the government gets to take off the top. Tax is a major expense and should be minimized legally as much as possible.

Remember:

INDIVIDUALS: Earn - Pay taxes - Live on the remainder

This is where owning a company comes in. Earnings are taxed last, which means the government only receives their share of your income last.

COMPANIES: Earn - Deduct expenses - Pay taxes on the remainder

Once you can master this concept and learn to legally and ethically maximize your deductions, the more you can save, the more you can invest, the more you can create streams of income, the sooner you can achieve financial security, and the more you can give back to those in need.

We've talked about taxes in general; now let's look at some specifics regarding business taxes to help you understand why **having a corporate structure in place can save you money and protect your assets**.

The fun and sad truth about owning a business is that the taxman always comes to take his piece of the pie. But **knowing how to legally reduce your tax burden as much as possible is one of the most important parts of running a business.**

Since most company owners cannot keep up with the tax laws, regular meetings with your tax advisor and accountant are integral to managing your tax responsibilities. To demonstrate how it works, here is a very simplified tax example:

You own a business selling pies. If you sell 10,000 pies in a year at $20 a pie, you will have a total (or gross) **income** of $200,000 for the year. Fortunately, a business's income tax is not based solely on gross income. Instead, it is based on net income after accounting for things like expenses and depreciation. One of the most basic expenses is Cost of Goods Sold **(COGS)**. This is the actual cost of the supplies used to produce the products that you are selling. In this example, COGS would include the eggs, flour, sugar, berries and other ingredients used to make the pies. If it takes $10 of supplies to produce each pie, your total COGS will be $100,000, and your total *taxable* income will be reduced to $100,000 for the year.

Sounds pretty simple, right? In reality, tax calculations become much more complicated. For example, how do you account for the employees whom you pay or the salary that you might pay yourself (if you are baking the pies)? What about the industrial oven that you bought or the kitchen space that you rent? What if you own a catering van? What if you took a prospective buyer to lunch to tell them about your pies and the services that you provide?

Each of these kinds of expenses has its own special rules that you should be familiar with, so let's take a look at each of them in more detail.

A. Business Expenses vs. Capital Expenses

Business and capital expenses are two of the most basic concepts that all business owners should understand. Business expenses generally comprise the largest portion of total expenses and tend to be simpler to account for, so we will discuss those first.

1. Business Expenses. Essentially the costs associated with conducting your trade or business, business expenses include things like COGS, salaries for employees, or the cost of renting a workspace or storefront. Most business expense items are consumable, such as the flour that goes into a piecrust, or are things that you rent, such as your workspace or your employees' time and expertise. In general, business expenses are tax-deductible and will count against your taxable income. While most business expenses are fairly straightforward, some options warrant further explanation.

> **Home Office Expenses**. If you work from home and regularly use part of your house exclusively for conducting business, you may be able to deduct part of the costs associated with the living space—including mortgage interest, utilities, and depreciation—as business expenses. One of the most common ways to do this is as a flat

percentage. For example, if you have a room that you use as an office that comprises 10 percent of the total square footage of the house, you may be able to deduct 10 percent of your utilities or insurance costs as a business expense. The rules regarding home-office expense deductions are very specific, so if you operate out of a home office, as many start-up small businesses do, be sure to *consult your tax advisor or accountant* about the options available to you.

Travel. In general, travel expenses may be deducted as business expenses only if they are directly related to your business and if you travel outside of your **tax home**. Your tax home is considered the entire city or general area in which your business or work is located. For example, if you live in Chicago and travel to New York for two days of meetings, you are allowed to deduct the cost of transportation to and from New York, along with the cost of the hotel room while staying there. If you decided that you want to stay an extra couple of days to sightsee while you are there, the costs of the hotel for the extra two days are not considered business expenses and are not deductible.

Entertainment. If you entertain a client, customer, or employee, you may be able to deduct some of the related costs as business expenses if they meet one of the two following tests:

> **Directly Related Test.** To meet the directly related test for entertainment expenses (including entertainment-related meals), you must meet these three criteria:
>
> - The main purpose of the combined business and entertainment was the active conduct of business.
>
> - You did engage in business with the person during the entertainment period.

- You had more than a general expectation of getting income or some other specific business benefit at some future time.

Associated Test. Even if your expenses do not meet the directly related test, they may meet the associated test. To meet this test for entertainment expenses, you must show that the entertainment is:

- Associated with the active conduct of your trade or business, and

- Directly before or after a substantial business discussion

Since *entertainment* can be treated as a *gift*, it is important that you know the gifting rules between government contractors and federal employees.

Transportation. These expenses relate to business transportation that occurs within your tax home—that is, the entire city or general area in which your business or work is located. These include the ordinary and necessary costs of:

- Getting from one workplace to another in the course of your business or profession

- Visiting clients or customers

- Going to a business meeting away from your regular workplace

- Getting from your home to a temporary workplace when you have one or more regular places of work. These temporary workplaces can be either within the area of your tax home or outside that area.

Daily transportation expenses incurred while traveling from your home to your regular place of business are generally not deductible.

Car Expenses. If you use your car for business purposes, you can generally deduct some of the expenses related to using your car. In most cases, you can use one of the following methods to calculate your deductible expenses:

Standard Mileage Rate. This is a standard amount that you may deduct per mile that you travel in your car for business purposes. If you want to use this method, you must use it in the first year that the car is available for business use. You may change to the actual car expense method in later years.

Actual Car Expenses. If you do not want to use the standard mileage rate, you are allowed to deduct actual expenses that you incur related to the business use of your car. Some examples of deductible expenses are:

- Depreciation

- Licenses

- Tolls

- Lease payments

- Parking fees

- Repairs

- Tires

If you use your car for both personal and business use, you must divide your expenses between the two uses. For example, if you drive 4,000 miles in a year for business purposes and 6,000 a year for personal use, you may deduct 40% of your actual car expenses.

I recommend keeping a detailed journal in your vehicle or on your portable electronic device to record the purpose of trips, odometer start and stop readings, and actual miles traveled. If you get audited, you can provide journal entries that support your expense reports and reimbursements.

2. Capital Expenses. Capital expenses are the cost of purchasing assets that your company will own and use for at least a year. This includes things like computers, an oven for baking pies, or even an automobile that is used primarily for business purposes. Accounting for capital expenses can be more complex than figuring business expenses, and the two methods that may be used to do so are depreciation and amortization.

Depreciation. When a business buys a fixed asset with a useful life of over a year, the total cost of the asset generally may not be deducted in the year that it is purchased. Instead, the cost is divided up by the total estimated life of the asset and a portion is deducted each year. For example, if you buy a $30,000 catering van with an expected useful life of fifteen years, you can write off $2,000 every year for fifteen years as depreciation.

The IRS website (**www.irs.gov/Businesses/Small-Businesses-&-Self-Employed/A-Brief-Overview-of-Depreciation**) offers clear guidelines regarding property depreciation. You can depreciate property if it meets *all* of the following requirements:

- It must be property you own.

- It must be used in business or held to produce income. You never can depreciate inventory because it is not held for use in your business.

- It must have a useful life that extends substantially beyond the year it is placed in service.

- It must have a determinable useful life, which means that it must be something that wears out, decays, gets used up, becomes obsolete, or loses its value from natural causes. You can never depreciate the cost of land.

Amortization. Similar to depreciation, amortization allows you to deduct certain capital expenses over a period of time. The IRS allows you to amortize the costs associated with:

- Starting a business, including the costs of researching a business idea and creating a legal entity

- Getting a lease on business property

- Intangible assets defined in section 197 of the Internal Revenue Code, including business licenses, permits, patents, trademarks, trade secrets, customer loyalty (goodwill), intangible value of physical items such as client lists, and accounting and inventory records

Action Steps For You

1. I'll just repeat what I said earlier in this chapter: I encourage you to go to the library and read (or better yet, buy for yourself) *Tax Savvy for Small Business* by tax attorney Frederick Daily. While this is written for the small-business owner, it clearly outlines year-round tax strategies to save you money and it does so in plain language that anyone can understand. There are many books like this that you can buy, but I personally found this book very helpful!

2. Make sure you have a great certified public accountant on your team who can help you understand the best ways to use every legal tax advantage available to you, whether you own a business or not. Meet with your accountant regularly, not just at tax time. You want to discuss your future plans with your accountant so they can advise you of tax impacts of your decision *before* you move forward with your plans. The advice they offer in advance may save you a lot of money and a lot of grief in the long run. I know too many people who only talk to their accountant at tax time and they miss out of the great advice they can get by keeping their accountant in the loop as finances grow.

3. Decide if you need a corporate structure in place, and if so, by all means set it up. If you are not sure how to do this, most accountants can advise you on how to do this, or they will do it for you for a fee.

4. Make it a priority to minimize your taxes legally and ethically in all areas of your life.

GIVE BACK

I have a sign on the wall just over my computer monitor that reads:

I Am Just A Steward

At the beginning of the book I said there are ten steps you should take to make sure you are well diversified and well on your way to securing your financial future. But this extra step is something you should be doing all the while you are working on steps 1-10: *give back*, and continue to give back more and more as you are able. You don't have to wait until you've completed all ten steps; get started today and boost your giving through the years as your investments grow.

I want to give my wife, Becky, full credit in this book. She is, quite simply, an amazing person. She is wired to be a caregiver and to give back.

I read over and over that the more people make, the more they become attached to their money and they tend to give back less and less, percentage-wise. I hope you will use your increased earnings as an excuse to give back *more and more.*

There are so many ways to *give back* to society, and it's not all about the money. Giving money can be a good thing, and as you increase your earning power, I hope you will consider giving back more and more from your streams of income. We strive to give back more than ten percent of our pre-tax income.

But besides giving more of your money, you can give back through your time, love, and other various resources. (But it has been interesting to me to learn and observe that as people make more and more money, often times they give back less and less of their resources, rather than more and more.)

Becky is a perfect example of how you can give back and often it does not take a lot of money. Sometimes through simple actions and just a little caring for others, you can make a big impact. And this is just one of the many reasons why I love her so.

> *Too often we underestimate the power of a touch, a smile, a kind word, a listening ear, an honest compliment, or the smallest act of caring, all of which have the potential to turn a life around.* — Leo Buscaglia

I believe everyone is put on this earth for a purpose. Becky's purpose is service to others — caregiving. If someone were to ask me to describe Becky, I could describe her by telling this story:

Whenever Becky walks into a cashier line at the local grocery store, one particular cashier's face lights up and the cashier can hardly hold back her excitement to see Becky.

One day when Becky was alone at the grocery store, Becky realized that the cashier was having a hard day, but the cashier was doing her best to put on a *good face* to the customers. You can often tell, I can often tell, and Becky, especially, has the ability to know how people are really feeling — when they need lifted up.

So, after having her groceries checked out by the cashier, Becky went over to the supermarket flower shop, bought a small bouquet of flowers, walked back over to give the bouquet to the cashier, and gave her a hug to let her know she was appreciated.

That describes my Becky. That one simple act defines Becky's heart. Becky is a caregiver, a person God put on this earth to care for others. Becky knows who she is and caregiving is what her heart longs to do most; it is just one way she gives back.

Yes, I was attracted to Becky for all of the reasons any guy is attracted to his first true love, but I noticed this compassionate, caring trait in Becky when she was just in junior high school (middle school). I loved that about her; I still love it about her. The best thing I can do for Becky is to enable her to live out her purpose — to be there for her and support her.

I have been blessed because she chose me to give her heart to — to care for.

Now, go out there and do like Becky and try to find a way to give back, to plant a seed that will grow and flourish and spread other seedlings while bringing you and your spouse even closer together.

As I said above, you don't have to wait until you have become rich to give back; all the while you are creating your streams of income you should:

> Command them to do good, to be rich in good deeds, and to be generous and willing to share. — 1 Timothy 6:18 (NIV)

Is there anything more special and satisfying to your soul than helping someone else out? Sometimes it is giving someone some flowers as Becky did; other times it is just a smile or a small gift.

> Every time you smile at someone, it is an action of love, a gift to that person, a beautiful thing. — Mother Teresa

That smile, that act of love or of helping or caring for others draws you closer to them and is just another way of giving back, and each time, you grow a little closer to God and to those around you.

Have you ever noticed that if you are in a funk or a bad mood or perhaps mad at someone close to you, how your spirit can be lifted by even the smallest act of helping or showing love to that someone?

> *I have found the paradox that if I love until it hurts, then there is no hurt, but only more love.* — Mother Teresa

So, when you are in a funk or in a bad mood, instead of brooding or seeking revenge, find a way to give back — plant a seed, be generous to that person. Create your own paradox. Be generous and love until it hurts; you will grow as a person and you will grow closer as a couple.

I can't say I have always been so giving. I was not wired like Becky to be so giving. But I have learned to plant seeds following Becky's lead.

In addition to supporting them financially, I have volunteered my *time* at a local homeless organization called The Lamb Center.

The Lamb Center exists to serve the poor and homeless in our community. They help the poor and homeless by feeding them, caring for them, and educating them so they can get back on their feet. The Lamb Center provides hot meals, hot showers, laundry service, haircuts, resume assistance, transportation assistance, access to phones and computers, legal assistance, dental and optical referrals, social security assistance, tax preparation assistance, access to medical and mental health specialists, and so much more.

At first, the thought of volunteering at the Lamb Center in Fairfax made me a little uneasy. I have always applied myself and worked very hard and I grew up with a biased belief that if people would just apply themselves, they too could get a job and make their own way.

But I had no idea of what it was like for the homeless until I started volunteering at the Lamb Center. I learned very quickly that being homeless, in most cases, has nothing to do with how hard someone does or does not work. But that is a whole separate story. Here, I want to talk about planting seeds.

How did I plant seeds at The Lamb Center? I volunteered my time, and I shared my life and business experiences. I helped the homeless finds jobs in several ways—I helped them create their resumes (sometimes they don't have even a draft resume, so we started from a blank sheet) or I helped them update their outdated resumes. I also helped them search for jobs online and, at times, apply online. One thing I did on an almost weekly basis for several years was search for published jobs that had came open in our local area that the homeless might have been able to apply for. Then the staff at The Lamb Center could put the job postings out for the homeless guests to check out as they passed through the center.

On one occasion, I met with a guest (at the Lamb Center we call the homeless visitors "guests") who had lost his job as a maintenance worker on a large horse farm just outside the city; he needed help writing his resume. More importantly, he needed a job. While he worked on the farm for those several years he was provided quarters to live in, but when he lost his job, he lost his place to live as well. It wasn't long before he became homeless as he exhausted his savings while looking for a new job.

I met with him, we talked about his past work experiences, and I created a resume for him from scratch. Next we searched online for several jobs he could apply for that he was qualified for, and I helped him upload his new resume and enter in all the personal information the companies needed to go with the resume. Then, I printed out several spare resumes for him to take with him as he left the Lamb Center to go on interviews.

All in all, I only spent a couple of hours with him. But I planted a seed. I gave back.

Often, in cases like this, after I have helped someone, I never hear from them again and I usually wonder if they got a job or if they just moved away.

In this case, about a year later I was at The Lamb Center talking to the staff when a man I did not initially recognize came up to me and started shaking my hand as he said, "You're the guy who helped me get a job! Thank you. Thank you. Thank you!" I smiled and then he hugged me as he told me about how he would never have found the job had I not taken the time to help him. I can't begin to tell you how great that felt.

I gave back, and my eyes water every time I remember that look on his face as he thanked me and shook my hand – over and over. My eyes are watering now as I type this.

You never know how just using the passions, skills, and gifts you have can affect someone else. Becky fully supports me as I use my God-given talents to give back in my own way. You grow individually as you give back and you grow closer to each other as you support your spouse in living out their purpose.

> *The person born with a talent they are meant to use will find their greatest happiness in using it.* – *Johann Wolfgang Von Goethe*

I hope you will use your talents and your resources and *give back*. Giving changes you in ways you will only understand when you give and see the impacts you can make on the lives of others. Don't just give money; think about Becky and the impact she made on the cashier. Think about the homeless guest at the Lamb Center who got a new job and is no longer homeless because of the one or two hours I spent with him to prepare his resume and apply for jobs.

We plan to donate from the profits of this book to support charities like the Lamb Center, so thank you in advance for buying this book.

Giving changes you, giving changes others, giving changes the world.

Action Steps For You

1. Give back!

2. Buy this book for your children and your friends who want to achieve financial security and could benefit from my life lessons.

3. Encourage everyone else you know who wants to achieve financial security to buy this book.

SOME FINAL THOUGHTS

Now you know my life-work story. I wanted to show you that if I can achieve financial security, even after working for twenty years without saving anything, you can achieve financial security too.

Now it's your turn. Take ownership of your finances. Map out your own plan. Diversify your learning and your investments, and create your future. But as you create your future:

Take ownership of your finances (Step 1)

Change the way you look at money (Step 2)

Recognize that you cannot learn everything (Step 3)

Make a commitment to never stop investing (Step 4)

Deal with your debt (Step 5)

Start an emergency fund (Step 6)

Start a company. Then start other companies (Step 7)

Diversify your assets (Step 8)

Protect your assets (Step 9)

Use every legal tax advantage you can to keep your money (Step 10)

Give back

A Final Action Step For You

If you learned from this book, please buy copies and share them with anyone you love that could benefit. You can help them start *now* to achieve their own *Financial Security in Ten Steps*.

APPENDIX A: BASICS FOR HOW TO START YOUR COMPANY

[This appendix is a summary of some of the more detailed material you can find in my book, *Start Grow Sell, A Primer for Starting, Growing and Selling Your Government Contracting Business. Start Grow Sell* is available on Amazon.]

This appendix details some of the key decisions you need to make, explains how to register with all the proper authorities (whether federal, state, or local), and teaches you how to prepare the proper internal documentation to help further legitimize your business. If you go step by step, you will see that start-up is not difficult to accomplish. The process can be time-consuming, but many steps can now be accomplished online.

You need to accomplish at least these ***fourteen key steps***:

1. Choose an Entity Type for Your Business
2. Order Materials from Your State
3. Choose a Name for Your Business
4. Establish a Logo and Website
5. Prepare and File Articles (Organization, Incorporation)
6. Choose a Management Structure
7. Prepare a Company Records Book
8. Prepare Either an Operating Agreement or Bylaws and Buy-Sell Agreement
9. Apply for a Federal Employee Identification Number
10. Set Up a Company Bank Account
11. Register with Your State Department of Taxation

12. Determine If Your Company Is Liable for Unemployment Tax
13. Apply for Business Licenses and Permits
14. Hold First Official Board Meeting

Now, let us look at each of those *fourteen key steps* in detail.

1. CHOOSE AN ENTITY TYPE FOR YOUR BUSINESS

One of the first steps in starting your own business is to decide what type of business structure you would like to use, and that decision will be largely dictated by the type of business you are going to create. The two most popular and widely used options are the Limited Liability Corporation **(LLC)** and the S Corporation **(S-Corp)**, so most of our discussion focuses on these two entity types. There are, however, several other options, including Sole Proprietorship, General Partnership, Limited Partnership, Limited Liability Partnership, Professional Corporation, and the C Corporation (regular corporation).

> We cannot overemphasize the importance of this decision, and we highly recommend you consult with a lawyer, accountant, and/or tax advisor to help choose which business structure is right for you—before you file any paperwork with the state. You can also see Step 9 in this book for an overview of each entity type.

2. ORDER MATERIALS FROM YOUR STATE

Once you decide on business structure, you should order the corresponding materials needed to stand up your business in the state that you decide to file in. In most cases, these materials can easily be found online. In Virginia, for example, the startup materials for an LLC can be found on the Virginia State Corporation Commission website (www.scc.virginia.gov/clk/dom_llc.aspx).

These materials include, but are not limited to, forms for filing your Articles of Organization, Reservation of LLC Name, and Statement of Change of Registered Agent.

Similarly, the startup materials for a corporation can be found at www.scc.virginia.gov/clk/dom_corp.aspx, and include forms such as Articles of Incorporation, Application for Reservation or for Renewal of Reservation of a Corporate Name, Guide for Articles of Merger, etc. A guide will accompany each of these forms with instructions on how to complete the form and where to send it.

To find your startup forms, simply do a web search for "[*your state's name*] state corporation commission." In most cases, you will be directly led to your state's site. There you typically can find a section called *Forms and Fees*, or even a *Start a Business* section that will have everything you need to get started.

3. CHOOSE A NAME FOR YOUR BUSINESS

When you decide on a business name, it cannot be a name that is already registered in your state. Although not absolutely necessary, it is also a good choice to avoid a name that is being used in any other state as well to avoid a potential conflict. You do not want your name to be even close to that of a national brand name, as these companies place a very high emphasis on protecting their names, trademarks, and copyrights. You can quickly check a potential name by conducting a web search. If you do not find any hits or close matches, you are probably on the right track.

You should try to think of several different options for a company name, just in case your first choice is already in use (and you would be surprised how often this is the case). When you have chosen a potential name (and some just-in-case options), you should immediately reserve the name with the state, on the off chance that someone else may be considering the same name and beat you to getting it. I have found the Virginia State Corporation Commission very helpful in this regard. I simply give them a call, and they perform a search to tell me whether or not the name is already in use, or if there is even a very similar name already in use.

> **As you choose a name for your business, make sure the name meets your state's naming requirements.**

These requirements vary by state and can usually be found in the state's Articles paperwork. You need to be aware of three main rules. First, a designator of some sort is typically required in your official name such as *Limited Liability Company, Incorporated, Limited,* or some abbreviation of one of these *(LLC, Inc., Ltd.,* etc.). Second, words that allude to the formation of certain kinds of business, such as banking and insurance, are often prohibited from being used in a company name unless you have the proper permits to operate in those fields. Finally, if you plan to operate a professional LLC or professional corporation, be aware most states have special naming requirements for these businesses, which include, but are not limited to, state-licensed professions in the fields of law, accounting, engineering, architecture, and medicine.

DBA or Doing Business As

Given the various naming requirements, many companies decide that they want to publicly use a name that is different from their official business name. For this purpose, they use what is called a Doing Business As **(DBA)** business name. You also commonly see this referred to as an assumed, fictitious, or trade name. For example, a bakery wants to have their storefront business operate under a different name than their official business name. In this case, they would simply reserve their legal name, we will call it *Baking Sciences, LLC,* with the state, and use that name to file their Articles. Next they could file an Assumed or Fictitious Business Name form with their state with the name *The Cupcake Factory*. This would allow them to put *The Cupcake Factory* on their storefront and operate publicly under that name, while maintaining the less appealing *Baking Sciences, LLC* as their legal name for official purposes.

Companies may opt to use a DBA simply for its ease of use. For example, the official name of one of my companies is Intelligence Consulting Enterprise Solutions, Inc., which is quite a mouthful. Instead, they use the DBA name ICES, which is a lot easier for people to remember and say. And besides, who wants to write all of that every time?

Legalities aside, once you pick a name for your company, you are going to use it for a long time. Your company name is often the first piece of information people learn about your business. For these reasons, you want to choose a name that is distinctive, appealing, and easy to remember. It's also a good idea to avoid specifics like your name, geographic location, or the name of the goods/services you will provide. For example, names like Steve's Stereos or Southwest Bakery can be both forgettable and limiting. What if you decide to expand your stereo store to sell TVs and computers, or you want to expand your bakery to the northeast side of town? You might come to regret choosing such a limiting name down the road. These are not ironclad rules, but they are good guidelines to keep in mind.

4. ESTABLISH A LOGO AND WEBSITE

You don't need to address a lot of marketing issues early in the startup process, but you do need to acquire a logo and establish a web presence. Simply having a polished logo for use on business cards, letterheads, email signatures, etc., can go a long way toward making you and your business look professional. For those of us who aren't particularly creative or artistic, it can be a great idea to team up with a graphic designer.

Designer and Motion Graphics Artist

I have a great relationship with David Kay (**www.davidkay.tv**), a designer and motion graphics artist exactly for this purpose. Whenever one of my business partners needs graphics, motion graphics or a logo, we pass along the name of the company and a description of the business to David Kay. After a brief discussion with the client, David puts

---

> together a few designs to choose from. If you
> have any color scheme preferences, be sure to
> share those preferences in initial discussions
> with your designer of choice. Otherwise,
> designers can give you direction with color
> choices as well.

Whether you design it yourself or outsource the work, a logo and a color scheme can also go a long way to getting started with designing a website. Even before you begin work on website design, you should reserve your domain name with GoDaddy or another domain registration service. Registration is fairly inexpensive, and it can save you the headache that can come if somebody beats you to a domain name. I usually use the .com domain, but like to also reserve .net and .org domains to block other companies from using them. Additionally, you can have the .net and .org domains redirect to your primary .com domain, so potential customers will find you no matter what they type.

If you neglect domain registration now and operate your business for a couple of years without a website, you may find that someone else reserved or is even using the domain that you want. This situation can get sticky and even expensive if you have to buy the domain name from them at an inflated price.

5. PREPARE AND FILE ARTICLES (ORGANIZATION, INCORPORATION)

The next step in the process is to file your articles with the state in which you will operate. For an LLC, you file **Articles of Organization**. For a corporation, you file **Articles of Incorporation**. Both types of articles usually consist of a simple one- or two-page form that asks for basic information such as your official business name, primary business address, and the name and information of the initial **registered agent,** whose sole purpose is to receive or forward any process, notice, or demand to the business entity. After the state reviews and accepts your articles, you will receive a certificate from the State Corporation Commission or similar governing agency certifying your existence as new business. Filing fees usually run around $100, and to maintain your status, you will pay annual registration fees of about the same amount.

6. CHOOSE A MANAGEMENT STRUCTURE

Companies that opt for an LLC structure must also choose a management structure for their business. The first and most common option is known as **member-managed**. For most small businesses, the owners, also known as **members**, are going to be directly involved in the day-to-day operations and management of the LLC. In this case, they will want to choose the member-managed format, which, in most states, is actually the default format. Smaller business can benefit from this structure because it eliminates an extra level of bureaucracy on overhead.

A second option, **manager-managed**, is for those companies that plan on bringing in outside investors who will be official members of the LLC, but who will not be involved in the day-to-day operations or management of the company. In this case, the company will want to designate one or more people as managers. These managers can be designated from within the pool of members, non-members hired specifically as managers, or a combination of both.

In some states, the initial members and managers are designated in the articles of organization and can be changed in the future by filing appropriate paperwork with your state. In other states, such as Virginia, one registered agent is named in the articles and members and managers are named later in an operating agreement. As the operating agreement is primarily an internal document (it is not filed with your state or any other governing body), it is easier to make changes among members or managers in the future.

7. PREPARE A COMPANY RECORDS BOOK

Law does not require an official company records book, but it is a good idea to have one for organizational purposes. Typically a simple binder, or perhaps a designated place in a filing cabinet located in your primary business office, it contains a copy of all of your most important organizational documents. These documents should be available for quick reference for internal purposes, as well as for an outside party that could require access to the information. The binder will contain just about everything needed to show you are operating as a legitimate business in the eyes of the government, including, but not limited to:

- A copy of your Articles
- State Corporation Commission certificate
- Operating Agreement or Bylaws
- Buy/Sell Agreement
- Federal Employee Identification Number **(EIN)**
- Local and state business licenses
- Initial and ongoing Meeting Minutes
- Stock Certificates and stubs
- Corporate Seal

> If you do not want to assemble a company records book yourself, a quick web search will display a number of companies that sell sample company records books. These books are usually specific to an LLC, S-Corp, etc., and come prepared with section dividers, blank stock certificates, and even various forms that you might find useful in your business.

8.   PREPARE EITHER AN OPERATING AGREEMENT OR BYLAWS AND BUY-SELL AGREEMENT

Once you complete filing Articles, you should put in place an operating agreement (if you are an LLC) or bylaws (if you are a corporation). These are both internal documents, put together and signed by the owners/members of a business, which lay out the rules and regulations for how the business will be run.

Here is a general overview of what goes into each kind of document so that you are aware of exactly what they are and what their purpose is. You can find fantastic books that walk you through preparing these documents, so I'll skip step-by-step instructions for what can be a lengthy process. After you prepare a draft, it is always a good idea to have a lawyer review it for what you might need to add or change. If you want to spend the money, you can have a lawyer prepare the entire document.

Operating agreements and bylaws cover similar topics but are different enough to warrant separate discussions. For an LLC, see 8a, *Preparing Your Operating Agreement*. For a corporation, move on to 8b, *Preparing your Bylaws and Buy/Sell Agreement*.

8a. Preparing Your Operating Agreement. An LLC Operating Agreement typically includes:

Preliminary Provisions. This section includes much of the same information found in your articles of organization, such as the name, address and state of formation of the LLC; the effective date of the operating agreement; information about the registered agent and office; and statement of your business purposes. The statement of purpose should be brief and concise, so it gives a good general idea of what your business will do without limiting the scope too much in case you want to expand down the road.

Membership Provisions. This section covers the basic rights and responsibilities of the members of the LLC. Information includes, but is not limited to: whether the LLC is member-managed; members' percentage interest and voting rights in the LLC; compensation of members; and members' meetings.

Manager Provisions (only necessary if manager-managed). If you choose to be a manager-managed LLC, this section lays out the rules and regulations for managers. It includes, but is not limited to: naming of managers; authority and voting rights of managers; information about management terms; provisions for managers' meetings; and, of course, provisions for the compensation of the managers.

Tax and Financial Provisions. This section establishes the tax classification for your LLC (partnership, sole proprietorship, or corporation) and the accounting method used (either cash or accrual). It also details how you will handle income tax returns and reports, as well as setting up bank accounts in the name of your business. While most LLC owners choose to be taxed as a partnership (or sole proprietorship, in the case of a single-member LLC), some choose to be taxed as an S-Corp or even a C-Corp. You should discuss this decision with your accountant, as there will be many tax implications to consider, and the decision should be documented appropriately in your official records.

Capital Provisions. This section discusses exactly how you will handle capital contributions, allocations, and distributions to and from members and the LLC.

Buy/Sell Provisions. This portion of the operating agreement can be very detailed and as lengthy as the rest of the sections combined. It lays out exactly what will happen if you decide to sell your business in whole or in part. It includes procedures for when an individual member decides to sell his or her membership interest in the LLC. This might not seem terribly important when first starting up, but it can also make life a whole lot easier when you have the ground rules laid out in advance, so there will be no room for conflict or confusion.

8b. Preparing Your Corporate Bylaws and Buy/Sell Agreement. For a corporation, the buy/sell agreement typically is a separate document from the bylaws. Here is an overview of the different sections typically included in the bylaws, followed by a brief summary of what goes into the buy/sell agreement.

Bylaw key sections may include:

1. Offices. States the physical address of the corporation's principal office.

2. Shareholders' Meetings. This section lays out guidelines for holding shareholders' meetings. It includes, but is not limited to: the location where meetings will be held; provisions for regular meetings, whether they be annual, quarterly, etc.; provisions for special meetings; information about how to give notice of meetings; voting procedures; and how to take action without holding a meeting.

3. Board of Directors. This section discusses everything pertaining to the Board of Directors **(BOD)** of the corporation, including but not limited to: powers of the BOD; the number, tenure, and election of directors; provisions for BOD meetings; and compensation for the directors.

4. Officers. This section details the rights and responsibilities of the various officers of the corporation. The officers most often defined in the bylaws are the President, Secretary, and Treasurer, but you may see other titles such as Vice President and Chairman of the Board. This section also lays out provisions for appointment, resignation, and removal of officers.

5. Executive Committees. If included in the bylaws, this section allows the BOD to appoint committees that report directly to the board. These committees can be given the power to approve corporate decisions in various designated business arcas on behalf of the board.

6. Shares. This section discusses topics relating to shares, such as issuing certificates and the issuance of shares.

Buy/Sell Agreement. As noted, this is typically a separate document from the bylaws, but it is similar to the buy/sell provisions found in an LLC operating agreement. The buy/sell agreement spells out all provisions for an owner to sell his/her interest in the company, as well as the rights of the company itself in this case. It also details provisions for the purchase of stock by the company in the case of a deceased owner.

9. APPLY FOR A FEDERAL EMPLOYEE IDENTIFICATION NUMBER

After you file Articles and have your basic paperwork in place, you should apply for a Federal Employer Identification Number **(EIN or FEIN)**, also known as a federal tax identification number. A very important number, it is basically the business equivalent to your personal Social Security number. It will be used to identify your business when filing tax returns, applying for business licenses, and opening bank accounts. The process for obtaining this is straightforward and can be accomplished online at the IRS website (www.irs.gov/Businesses/Small-Businesses-&-Self-Employed/Apply-for-an-Employer-Identification-Number-(EIN)-Online)

After you finish the application process online, your EIN will typically be emailed in a matter of minutes. Once received, you should print out several copies. One copy (at a minimum) goes in your company records book, and you need physical copies when you open a company bank account.

10. SET UP A COMPANY BANK ACCOUNT

When you have a federal EIN, you can set up your company bank account. Ideally, you will find a small-business-friendly bank that charges minimal fees, or even better, no fees at all. You can usually find a bank that forgoes monthly fees as long as you maintain a minimum monthly balance. Another factor to consider is that at some point, your company will probably want to open a line of credit **(LOC),** so be sure to do your research and talk to several banks. Before making a final decision, ask yourself if this bank is where you want to open your LOC.

> **Be prepared when you go to the bank to set up your business account!**
>
> When you are ready to set up your bank account, you need to bring several things, including personal identification, your SCC certificate, and proof of your business EIN. You also need money for your initial deposit. Something to keep in mind is whether or not you want overdraft protection for your account. The two main types of overdraft protection are by attaching either a savings account or a credit card to your main checking account. If you decide to open a savings account, be sure to have extra cash on hand to deposit in it.

11. REGISTER WITH YOUR STATE DEPARTMENT OF TAXATION

No matter where your business will operate, you must know and comply with your state and local tax laws. For example, virtually all states levy income taxes. C corporations and LLC owners who elect the corporate tax treatment are taxed on their income separately from their owners. S corporations, sole proprietors, partnerships, and LLC owners that elect the sole proprietorship or partnership tax treatment are treated as pass-through entities, in which case, the owners list the business income on their personal taxes. You can go to the SBA website for a complete listing of the information you need to register for taxes by state (www.sba.gov/content/learn-about-your-state-and-local-tax-obligations).

12. DETERMINE IF YOUR COMPANY IS LIABLE FOR UNEMPLOYMENT TAX

If you do not plan to have employees, then you do not have to address unemployment tax liability immediately. Requirements vary by state, and you should read them, so you'll be prepared if you later decide to hire employees. To give you a general idea of whether or not you may need to register for state unemployment tax, here are the Virginia requirements.

Your business is subject to unemployment tax if it meets one or more of the following conditions:

- Has at least one employee (ten for agricultural business) for some portion of any day, in each of twenty different weeks in a calendar year.

- Has $1,500 in total gross quarterly payroll ($20,000 agricultural business or $1,000 for domestic labor) in any calendar quarter.

- Has acquired another business subject to the tax.

- Is a governmental operation or political subdivision.

- Is a non-profit organization and has four or more employees for some portion of a day during any twenty different weeks in a calendar year.

> You can find specific requirements on each state employment commission website, and in most cases you can register for the tax electronically.

13. APPLY FOR BUSINESS LICENSES AND PERMITS

There are a number of different federal, state, and local licenses that you may be required to hold in order to operate your business legally. Agriculture, aviation, firearms, commercial fishing, and transportation are just a few industries that require special licenses to operate. Even if you only want to operate your business from a home office, you will likely need a permit to do so. A quick and easy way to figure out which licenses and permits may be required is to use the SBA's Permit Me tool (www.sba.gov/licenses-and-permits). You simply enter your city/state or zip code and your business type, and the site gives you all the information you need to obtain the proper licenses and permits.

14. HOLD FIRST OFFICIAL BOARD MEETING

Part of running your business will be holding board meetings and having the Board Secretary keep official minutes of those meetings. These meetings can be held on a regular basis, such as annually or quarterly, or you can hold meetings as the need arises. Additionally, meetings can be held in person, virtually, or purely on paper. The main purpose of board meetings is to document important decisions made on behalf of the company.

At a minimum, your first meeting minutes should account for the following decisions:
1. Appoint a chairperson
2. Appoint officers
3. Establish a principal office
4. Discuss/approve the operating agreement
5. Approve opening a company bank account
6. Authorize payment for startup costs.

After you hold your first board meeting, a number of other situations would typically call for a documented board meeting to take place. These situations include, but are not limited to:

1. Amending your operating agreement or bylaws
2. Amending your articles of organization/incorporation
3. Approving significant purchases, such as real estate
4. Selling of major LLC assets
5. Selling or expanding divisions of the company
6. Adding of a new member
7. Voting on any other matters that require approval by the members or shareholders, including important legal, business, financial, or tax decisions

ABOUT THE AUTHOR

My hope is that by reading this book you will know more about me and my work and you will understand the experiences that ultimately shaped my business strategies and my investment strategies.

I love what I do, and if you are willing to work hard and to think unconventionally, then you, too, can escape the 8-to-5 grind, and create your own path to *Financial Security in Ten Steps*.

My background includes 20 years in the Air Force as a systems acquisition expert followed by 20+ years as a government contractor, business owner and business consultant and now author and amateur photographer.

After 20 years in the Air Force, I found myself living almost paycheck-to-paycheck and I had very little money set aside for retirement or for emergencies. I was nowhere near financial security and it began to worry me.

I was worried enough that I spent the next 20+ years building a diversified portfolio that provides us financial security going into our upcoming retirement years. This book is not a get-rich-quick story. This book, written primarily to my three children, is my personal story about the ten steps I took to create my diversified portfolio and achieve financial security.

I want my children to know these ten steps and to understand that if they are to achieve financial security, they need to *take ownership* of their own financial situation like I did and *create* their own financial security. Financial security is an individual responsibility. You cannot pass this responsibility off to your financial advisor or your broker or your spouse. You need to take ownership of your own future and your own finances like I did.

After I wrote the first draft of this book I asked a few people to read the draft and give me feedback. I was excited to learn that others were encouraging me to share this book to a wide audience and not just limit this book to my children.

My hope is that anyone that wants to achieve financial security can learn from this book.

About My Work

After retiring from twenty years in the Air Force, I went on to serve in executive management positions with annual revenues of up to $160 million, including Corporate Vice President at SAIC, President and COO of McClendon Corporation, and President at Intelligence Consulting Enterprise Solutions, Inc., providing support to various U.S. government agencies.

In 2013, I started The Unconventional Strategist to provide one-on-one business and management consulting services to companies of all sizes. My specialties and background include business startup and consulting, executive consulting-coaching, systems engineering, and systems integration in the commercial market as well as the Department of Defense (DOD), and Intelligence Community (IC) sectors.

I consult primarily as a business coach and mentor. The company name says it all; I work with you, or with you and your executive team, to help strategize and think "unconventionally" about growing personally and professionally. I can help you map out a plan to start, grow and even sell your company — if that is your goal.

Additionally, I have ownership in multiple businesses that I founded or co-founded that operate in the commercial, DOD and IC markets. You can own one or more companies, too, if that is what you chose to do. I admit, it takes hard work, and it takes time. It also requires putting together a strategy, which is just one of the things I can help you with through The Unconventional Strategist.

When I look back over my twenty years in the Air Force, I never gave much thought to owning my own business, let alone owning more than one. Instead, I focused on doing the best I could in whatever job I had. When I became a contractor, I started to get the entrepreneurial bug and to think about owning my own business and setting my own agenda.

This book is the story of my personal journey as I set my own path, followed my own agenda, created my own businesses and ultimately achieved *Financial Security in Ten Steps*.

Tommy Keith

www.ingramcontent.com/pod-product-compliance
Lightning Source LLC
Chambersburg PA
CBHW021425170526
45164CB00001B/97